D1065560

∴ THE GOLDEN THREAD ∴

The Golden Thread

Storytelling in Teaching and Learning

by
Susan Danoff

The Golden Thread:
Storytelling in Teaching and Learning
by Susan Danoff

Storytelling Arts Press
A Division of Storytelling Arts, Inc.
First Edition, 2006
Copyright © 2005 Susan Danoff

Printed in the United State of America

Library of Congress Control Number: 2006900052

ISBN 0-9777228-0-5
  978-0-9777228-0-8

Contents:
1. Education   2. Storytelling
3. Social Skills 4. Imagination   5. Literacy
6. Language Arts 7. Folktales

Book design by Sue Bannon
Cover illustration by Leslie Danoff

 Storytelling Arts Press
Post Office Box 135
Kingston, NJ 08528-0135
info@storytellingarts.net
www.storytellingarts.net

to
my father, Neal, and Jonah
and in memory of my mother
for their teachings of
love, wisdom, and imagination

⋮ TABLE OF CONTENTS ⋮

⋅⋅⋅ ACKNOWLEDGEMENTS ⋅⋅⋅

MY LONG-TIME Storytelling Arts friends and colleagues have participated in numerous discussions about the practice and meaning of storytelling in school classrooms. I am very grateful to all of them for helping me to understand these issues more deeply through their artistry and thoughtfulness as storytellers and teachers: Paula Davidoff, Helen Wise, Tara McGowan, Joanne Epply-Schmidt, Luray Gross, Ellen Musikant, Jim Rohe, Julie Della Torre, Julie Pasqual, Joy Vrooman Sayen, Nadine Grisar, and Mary Rachel Platt. Collaboration with Teresa Whitaker each summer at our Vermont storytelling retreat has nourished my spirit and love for stories.

I am particularly grateful to Tara McGowan for reading *The Golden Thread* several times and offering suggestions for revision. Her work as a researcher for Storytelling Arts has helped me to understand some of these issues more clearly, and several of the quotations from teachers come from her interviews. Margie Thurman, Eliza McFeely, and Kitsi Watterson encouraged me throughout the process, and Marni Gillard not only offered much needed encouragement from afar but provided valuable guidance about publishing the manuscript.

Terry O'Connor allowed me to audit his class on the sociology of education at The College of New Jersey. Through Terry's class I gained insight into the profound impact of storytelling on classroom culture. Workshops with David Grant and Grant Wiggins helped me to identify the big ideas in educational storytelling.

Many school administrators have also collaborated with me over the years, opening their doors to our program. In particular I would like to recognize the contributions of Jane Fremon, Julia Rhodes, Barbara Tedesco, Edna Margolin, Diane Cyr, Marie Leonessa, Llionel Henderson, and Dennis Levinson. The teachers and students who have willingly welcomed me into their classrooms are too numerous to name, but I wish to thank them all.

Marue Walizer and John Webb, past and current directors of the Teacher Preparation Program at Princeton University, have given Storytelling Arts the opportunity to run our summer institutes at Princeton. I developed many of the ideas in this book by working intensively with teachers at the institute.

The board members of Storytelling Arts, past and present, have helped to grow the organization and expand the reach of storytelling in education. My thanks go to Sandy Millspaugh, Dan Gardiner, Marue Walizer, Willa Spicer, Eliza McFeely, Wes Thurman, Carol Brown, Lillian Burke, Holly Houston, Karin Clark, Margorie Gutman, Kitsi Watterson, Ellen Goellner, Ellen Frede, Helen Wise, Paula Davidoff, and the late Judy Trachtenberg. My dear friend Elliott Lee helped me begin Storytelling Arts as first board president by guiding me into the world of nonprofits and foundations. Our ongoing discussions have helped me gain more clarity and understanding about how our work fits into a bigger picture.

The foundations that have supported Storytelling Arts since 1998 have allowed us to take our work into classrooms for extended periods of time, enabling us to work out new strategies and reach children with special needs. Special thanks go to the Epply Charitable Foundation, the Geraldine

R. Dodge Foundation, the Educational Foundation of America, the Mary Owen Borden Foundation, and the Princeton Area Community Foundation. The late Susan J. Epply's generous gift gave Storytelling Arts the opportunity to exist, expand, and take our programs into the world. Without her vision, our work could not have moved forward. Scott McVay, David Grant, Robert Perry, and Ross Danis of the Dodge Foundation and Tom and John Borden of the Borden Foundation have collaborated with us on a long-term basis, helping us serve children in poverty.

My first two storytelling teachers, Diane Wolkstein and Laura Simms, provided the initial spark for my love of the oral tale, a spark that has never burned out. My friend Dudley Carlson, the former children's librarian at the Princeton Public Library, gave me my first opportunities to share stories in public and has been my guide and mentor in the world of children's literature throughout my adult life.

This book would not look as it does without the artistry of two women who made me feel as if they took an ordinary girl and dressed her in beautiful robes: Sue Bannon who designed the book and my sister Leslie Danoff who painted the lovely watercolor on the cover. Leslie and Storytelling Arts Business Manager Vicki Becker also meticulously copyedited the manuscript.

In fairytales, there is sometimes a character who just appears magically to help the protagonist. This character stands for pure generosity. Ever since I founded Storytelling Arts, such helpers have appeared to propel our work forward. I am very grateful to those who have appeared in this magical way to help Storytelling Arts: Joanne Epply-Schmidt, Susan J. Epply, David Ehrenfeld, Claire Jacobus, and Pam

Carter. My dear friend and master storyteller Ann Lee Brown has been an inspiration throughout my career and is the special friend and good fairy who has helped Storytelling Arts produce this book.

My parents bequeathed to me a love for books, social consciousness, and a profound respect for teaching and learning. If it were not for their ability to listen and ask questions, I don't think I would have become a storyteller.

I met my husband Neal just as I embarked upon the path of storytelling in 1979. He has offered only encouragement throughout the past twenty-six years. Our discussions about teaching, literature, and writing have enabled me to continue on this path, even when I wasn't sure I could. He was very patient in rereading drafts of this manuscript and repeatedly told me not to give up.

My son Jonah has always been willing to listen to a story. My favorite moments during the past thirteen years have been just before his bedtime, when I have told him stories and read him all of the literature I have loved since I was a child. His imagination and understanding of language are gifts that I hope will always sustain him.

∴ PREFACE ∴

For over twenty-five years I have been telling stories, using stories to teach emergent literacy and writing, and helping teachers become storytellers in their own classrooms. This book has grown out of my belief that storytelling is not an entertaining diversion, a filler, a treat on a cloudy day, or a reward for good behavior. Nor is it a craft that belongs solely to the professional storyteller who visits classrooms on special occasions. Storytelling is a method of teaching, a way to gain trust, to communicate effectively, to inspire imaginative thinking, and to provide a foundation for the thinking that is basic to literacy.

The Golden Thread lays a foundation for understanding what is really happening in children's learning when we teach through stories. In a book about storytelling it is important to be reminded of the magic of the tale. For that reason I have begun each section with a story that serves as a metaphor for the discussions that follow. The essays at the heart of the book reflect upon the unique capacity of storytelling to teach, what we're teaching when we tell stories, and why it seems to work.

I begin by considering the role of teacher as storyteller. Teachers are unusually well equipped to tell stories because of their already finely honed communication skills. Once they have stories in their repertoire, using those stories can profoundly affect social interaction – the relationship of teacher to student and the building of class community.

Stories not only address social and behavioral issues in

the classroom as I discuss in Part II; they also help children to think. Stories links feelings and thoughts, and the place of intersection is the imagination. Part III, "Storytelling and Imagination," shows us how stories can perform a great service to the child's developing imagination because they hone the skills of visualizing, envisioning, and play that help us to become thinkers and actors in the world.

Some teachers and storytellers believe that our work has the greatest impact on children's literacy. I have saved my discussion on literacy for Part IV because I believe that the behavioral issues and the development of imaginative thinking are prerequisites to literacy. In schools where children struggle with literacy, often for cultural reasons, storytelling can have a profound influence on learning to read and write.

Finally I talk about the spirit of the teacher. Storytelling can feed our spirits and remind us why we became teachers in the first place. It can place us among the vast chain of teachers since ancient times who have compelled their students to learn through the sheer power of the story to captivate, inspire, and transform the imagination.

My Personal Journey As a Storyteller and Teacher

I have loved stories ever since I can remember. As the youngest in a family of readers, I was the very last to learn to read. One of my earliest memories is my first day of first grade, the year my mother had told me I would learn to read. I came home from school that day deeply disappointed because I had not learned this magical skill and announced, "If I don't learn to read tomorrow, I'm quitting school."

It was not many days before I became an avid reader, and books have been my constant companions ever since. As I recall it now, my longing for stories was an insatiable hunger. I spent as much time as I possibly could reading books. I didn't just read them; it felt as if I ate and drank them. I devoured them.

My mother took my sister and me to the library once a week, and we were allowed four books each. For years I kept careful records of what I read, often making up codes for how I felt about them. Although I had favorites, I was usually in love with whatever conjured my imagination at the time.

But it was never enough for me just to read a book; I always had to tell someone the story of what I had read. For the experience to be complete, I needed to pass on the gift.

When I was in the eighth grade in 1966, the town of Wilkes-Barre, Pennsylvania set up a tutoring program as part of the Office of Economic Opportunity, a group of social programs for the poor. I don't know why the program was willing to accept a thirteen year old as a volunteer tutor, but they agreed to try me out, and I stayed on through high school.

My first student, Robert, was a small white boy in the fifth grade. The first day I sat down with him at a card table in the dark basement of the YMCA, he looked me in the eye, put his fist on the table, and said, "I just want you to know right now, I'm a slow learner."

You might imagine that this was quite a stunning remark to hear in my very first moment as a teacher. Though I cannot remember exactly how I responded, I know that I attempted to dismiss his sense of failure and focus him on the task at hand.

The first thing that I did was to try to determine what Robert knew. I had some children's books with me, but he couldn't read a word. I discovered that though he could recognize some of the letters of the alphabet by name, he didn't know that letters were symbols and that words signified meaning. In fact, he thought that reading was magic: some people could do it and some people couldn't. He was just one of those that the magic hadn't touched.

I taught Robert the sounds of the letters quickly and easily, and he began to see how to form them into the magic of words. His family moved away from Wilkes-Barre about six months later. For years I regretted that I couldn't take him further, though I always hoped that at least he knew that he had the capacity to learn, and that reading was a code that he could break.

I learned from teaching Robert that if a child carries within him the belief that he cannot learn, and if no one believes in his ability, it is doubtful that he will learn.

My second student was more difficult than Robert. Trina was an African-American child in a largely white community. I would often board the bus and take a half hour bus ride to the Y, only to discover that Trina hadn't shown up that day.

Trina was in the third grade. Like Robert, she could not read; in addition, she *would* not read. I recall our first session. We were sitting on the side bleachers in the empty YMCA gym when Trina said, "I don't need to read."

My mind began to work quickly to think of all the reasons why reading would help her. I began with the most practical I could think of. "What if you want to look up someone's phone number in a phone book?"

"I'll ask someone," she said.

"When you're older, what if you want to drive somewhere and you can't read the street signs?"

"I'll take someone with me."

Looking up at the red exit signs on either side of the gym, I said, "How would you know how to get out of a building if you can't read that sign over there?"

"I'll just go out the door, " she said.

I cannot recall how many other reasons I came up with, but Trina had an easy rebuttal for every one of them.

I gave up on that strategy. Instead, I began to bring picture books to our sessions and read to her. Eventually she dropped her resistance and learned to read. Many years later I found out that she had gone to college.

These early experiences taught me, first of all, that I was absolutely hooked on teaching. They also taught me that the obstacles to learning often have little to do with learning itself. Those moments of breaking through made even the futile bus rides worthwhile.

If I had been wildly successful as a teenage tutor, I was a dismal failure as a middle school English and social studies teacher. In 1979 I took a job in a very small New Jersey community where I was responsible for sixth, seventh, and eighth grade social studies, English, drama and a few other subjects. I also threw in Chinese as a bonus, and with the greatest enthusiasm only a young teacher can have, I embarked on a job that required ten preparations a day.

It wasn't the preps that destroyed me, though. It was the kids. About half my class had parents who were going through divorces; a boy named Greg had a father in jail and liked to throw things; Tommy still peed in his pants; and a pair of obstreperous twins would not even follow the principal when he asked them to leave the classroom with him. There was so much anger in the class that it was like walking through pea soup. To top it off, the students had idolized the male teacher who had just left and were determined to despise anyone who took his place. That was me.

A more seasoned teacher could have probably sorted it out, but I was a novice and not up to the task. There was, in fact, only one time during the day when the children would sit and listen, and that was when I read to them. I read them the whole of *Black Boy* by Richard Wright, and even though they were white children who had not undergone the deprivation of Wright, they deeply identified with his embattled childhood. The only punishment that had any sway with these children was my steadfast refusal to read *Black Boy* if they misbehaved. These were the only peaceful moments in that classroom, the only moments of community.

I put every ounce of energy I had into the job, all my

waking moments, seven days a week trying to make it work. One of my colleagues, still an educator these many years later, told me she cried every day after school during the year when she had taught the same children. Another friend, a retired career teacher who was then eighty years old, counseled me by saying, "You need to quit that job or you will never teach again." I left the job at Christmas.

But something else had happened to me that fall which was not unlike Alice falling through the rabbit hole. Another world had opened up for me just as the world of teaching seemed to be closing over me. I heard my first storyteller. One evening Diane Wolkstein told stories at the Princeton Public Library, not from a book, but from her heart, inviting us into a magical space where the story resided. I experienced an almost seamless transition from the every day world to the world of story. During the entire time she told her tale, I lived within it while all sense of ordinary time and space receded. Yet when the story was over, the vividness of the tale remained with me and resides in me still after twenty-five years. I had fallen, head first, into the world of storytelling. Although I did leave my middle school job, I have never left the teaching profession. Since that time I have been an itinerant teacher, and the wares that I carry are the many stories I keep in my invisible bag.

While I was working as a storyteller for the New Jersey State Council on the Arts in the 1980's, I happened to be placed in two long-term residencies in Trenton schools. These were schools with large minority populations in poor urban areas where children generally struggle with literacy and where the high school dropout rate is very high. Two particular incidents made an indelible impression on me.

At one school I had a group of fifteen fourth and fifth grade students who were selected to learn to be storytellers, and among them were a number of boys who could barely read and were considered discipline problems. They lit up for storytelling and put their hearts and souls into it. One was a tall fourth grader named Ronnie. Because Ronnie's reading skills were very weak, I taped the story he selected, and he read along with the text as he listened to the story on my walkman. Some weeks later during a tutorial session with Ronnie, I asked him, "Do you like to tell stories?" He replied, "Yes, but I *really* like to read." I was quite surprised by this and wanted to hear him read. We got out a folktale from the school library that he hadn't read before, and he began to read with fluency and understanding. Something magical had happened in that few weeks. Ronnie, who had been reading only words, suddenly realized that words strung together to make sense. Through storytelling he was able to reconstruct meaning from text just as he was able to create meaning in the oral telling of his own tale.

In another class, a seventh grade, I had a student named Felicia who sat in the back with her head down. I thought this child would never look up or lift her pencil. One day I told the African-American story *The People Could Fly*, and we talked about the emotional truth in this folktale, which captures the misery and cruelty of slavery and the indestructible desire for freedom. During the story, Felicia looked up. When the students wrote personal stories that mirrored the painful emotions in this story, Felicia picked up her pencil for the first time. She wrote, "I felt like pain. I was weak. I was tired. My heart was burning in flames of pain. Teardrops rolled down my cheek. They rolled into my mouth. I tried to hold my tears back. But I couldn't. They would just burn my eyes. The place was cold. The words that came out of my aunt's mouth were words of hurtness. My mother tried to hold her tears back. But I knew she wanted to cry. Her eyes looked like madness." When the children were required to write evaluations at the end of the year, Felicia wrote, "I liked the stories and sometimes I even liked myself."

Although most students I had visited in the past had welcomed me, the enthusiasm and appreciation that these children showed was far beyond anything I had ever experienced in a classroom. It confirmed my feeling that storytelling was a key in education, particularly in schools where children were failing miserably in the area of literacy. Because of Ronnie, Felicia, and many other wonderful students in Trenton, I decided that the storytelling I was doing through the State Arts Council was not enough. I looked into how to begin a nonprofit corporation, and in 1996 I founded Storytelling Arts, Inc., because I felt it was imperative that storytellers reach more low-income school children and speak to them through stories as I had spoken to Ronnie and Felicia. In founding the nonprofit, I also felt that if we could place storytelling in the hands of more teachers, we might transform the education of these children.

Since 1997 Storytelling Arts has given me the opportunity to work with twelve of my colleagues, bringing storytelling programs to New Jersey schools. All of our projects are long-term, since we are interested, not in the entertainment value of storytelling, but in its profound ability to teach.

I have also trained many teachers in the art of storytelling at our annual summer institutes at Princeton University and at numerous teacher workshops. This work has convinced me that teachers can easily and naturally learn to tell stories and to incorporate them into their work. The teachers I have worked with over the years have used storytelling extensively in their classrooms—teaching children to tell, teaching writing, and even teaching math.

The foundations that have funded our work have required that we collect data and assess the impact of storytelling on children's learning. This has prompted us to ask some challenging questions about what we do. Although it is obvious to anyone who observes a storytelling session that children are deeply engaged, it is important that we ask what they are learning and why it matters.

In our long-term projects, teachers have helped us to assess the impact of storytelling on their students, and I have included some of their comments. In thousands of observation forms that teachers have filled out over the past six years, we see several recurring themes. Teachers all over New Jersey at every grade level have told us they are surprised to see that their shy children speak during storytelling sessions; the children who are usually distracted, distracting, and inattentive seem to be able to focus when they listen to stories; and children who speak a language other than English are willing to engage and participate. The teachers are also surprised that their students remember the stories in detail, even after a very long period of time has elapsed. Some have reported that their reluctant writers are eager to write after they hear a story, and others have said that their students are more eager to read, especially if it's a story like the one they heard from the storyteller.

I am writing this book because when a teaching method has that much impact, particularly on the children who are most difficult to reach, every teacher needs to know about it. I also believe that storytelling is a teaching method available to any teacher who takes the time to learn and understand it.

Since I was thirteen years old, my work as a teacher has been a constant process of revelation, unfolding, and transformation. My students Robert, Trina, Ronnie, Felicia, and many others have inspired me along the way to focus on the most elusive aspects of teaching and learning: the desire to open oneself to the process of learning, to believe in one's own potential, to engage the heart and the mind together. Looking back, I realize that even before I had been introduced to storytelling, reading to Trina and to my difficult middle school students was the most effective way of reaching them that I knew. Storytelling, when I discovered it, became an even more powerful way to do so.

For me, storytelling is not only an art form but a handmaiden to teaching. That is something the ancients knew when they enveloped their values and beliefs, their hopes and fears, in the garment of story. It is something the religions of the world have always known as they transmitted metaphors of the life of the spirit through narrative. But it is something that our institutions of learning have forgotten. Indeed, storytelling is a language that children understand from an early age. It is the language of teaching. In the following pages I hope to be able to share how and why storytelling can change the intellectual and emotional life of a child.

PART I

TEACHER *as* STORYTELLER

The FORGOTTEN GIFTS

A LONG TIME AGO when rulers had great power and their subjects bowed their heads and obeyed, there lived a king who was sadder than sad. He was wrapped in gloom, and it seemed that the air hung heavy over his whole kingdom. He never smiled and rarely spoke except to give orders. No one knew why, and of course they feared to ask him. It had been this way for a long time, so long that people forgot it could be any different.

In spite of his dark temperament, the king had amassed a great amount of wealth through the hard work and imagination of his people. But this king's wealth was not just the ordinary kind. He had stables and barns filled with food and livestock and the usual treasure chests of gold and jewels, but he had even more than this. His palace was filled with the most magnificent and unusual objects. This is the story of how they came to be there.

EACH YEAR when the light stayed longest in the sky, the king would demand that his subjects bring him three gifts, gifts the likes of which he'd never seen before. And on that longest day when the sun was at the height of its journey across the kingdom, all the subjects would gather before the king in his courtyard. He would sit on his throne and receive the three gifts, while all the people would gasp in astonishment at their beauty and the striking ingenuity of the creators.

Once they gave him a full-length cloak made all of feathers, each one a different color; and a tusk of ivory onto which they'd carved in minutest detail the figures of a hundred children; and an enormous cake in the shape of the palace.

As for the king, he would receive the gifts but say nothing, his face like stone, for the glitter and inventiveness did not break through his dark countenance. He would hold each object in his hand, touch it, and take it back to the palace.

BUT A TIME came when jewelers had used every jewel and the carpenters every bit of precious wood; the cooks had made every flavor of cake and the goldsmith and silversmith had carved every design they could conceive and were empty.

All the people came together on the shortest day of the year as they always had and could think of no gifts that would help them survive the longest day.

For if they had no gifts, the king threatened to take three subjects as his own and make them into gifts for himself: a servant, a mistress, or maybe he'd just say, "A fine day for a hanging."

That year, call it what you will—an absence of riches, a drought of imagination, an emptiness of spirit. Whatever it was, there were no gifts to be made for the king. And every subject risked the chance that he or she would become the gift of sacrifice for the king.

ON THE DAY before the longest day of the year, the daughter of the goldsmith and the daughter of the jeweler and the daughter of the silversmith got together and they said, "We will bring the king his gifts this year."

Their parents asked, "What are they? We are poor and have nothing of value."

And the daughters answered, "We cannot say, but isn't it better you trust us than risk three lives?"

They hesitated but finally agreed.

THAT YEAR on the longest day the king sat as usual on the throne in his great courtyard and the citizens gathered. The three daughters came forward, but they held nothing in their hands, nor did they bear burdens on their backs, and they carried no small tokens in their pockets. This time the crowd gasped — not in astonishment — but in fear.

THE DAUGHTER of the goldsmith stepped forward first and she said, "For my gift I shall need the space of the earth. One hundred people must link arms and my gift will fill their circle." And one hundred people linked arms and the daughter of the goldsmith stepped into the circle.

The light of the longest day filled the circle and the daughter of the goldsmith spread out her arms and lifted her feet and she began to dance. Her fluid motion filled the circle, her skirts whirled into ribbons of designs, and the people felt they were floating with her on invisible currents of the wind.

When she had finished, the people regarded her with awe, for as long as the gloom had touched their king and their kingdom, they had forgotten how to dance. But when they recalled the king's demand for three gifts, they were fearful again. For when the dance was completed, there was nothing to hold, nothing to touch, nothing to take home to the palace.

But the daughter of the goldsmith put out her hand to the king and she said, "Come, your majesty. Come and dance with me." She reached for his hand and he stepped down from his great throne into the space of that enchanted circle, and he began to dance with the daughter. At first his steps were awkward and heavy, as if he hadn't yet discovered the magic in his own feet, but following her lead, he began to lift his feet and his arms, and soon they were whirling and twirling. And when they were finished and the king mounted the steps to his throne, he looked somehow different, as though the heaviness that clung to his robes was gone.

NEXT THE DAUGHTER of the jeweler stepped forward and she said, "For my gift I shall need the space of the air," and so saying, she began to sing.

As she sang the butterflies lit on the tops of the grass blades and listened, and the people seemed to forget they breathed, so caught were they by the sound that floated on the breeze. Her voice touched places that the living hand cannot reach.

When she had finished, the people regarded her with awe, for as long as the gloom had touched their king and their kingdom, they had forgotten how to sing. But when they recalled the king's demand for three gifts, they were fearful again. For when the song was completed, there was nothing to hold, nothing to touch, nothing to take home to the palace. And the people bent their heads further to the ground and feared to look up into the face of the king. But if they had, they would have seen that his face held a look of wonder.

Then the daughter of the jeweler stepped up to the king and she said, "Your majesty, with your permission, may we all sing together?"

And he nodded.

She sang a line, and they sang it back, tentatively at first and softly, then louder and more boldly. And as they sang, the king's voice, once dark and filled with gloom, became deep and sonorous and felt like a plush carpet on which all the other voices sang.

When they finished singing, the subjects all looked at their king, not with fear but with awe, and they saw a light had come into his once shadowed eyes.

AND THEN THE daughter of the silversmith stepped forward and she said, "Come close, my friends, for I need no space for my gift. I only need you to come as close as you can." And this daughter began to tell a story.

As she spoke the people traveled with her to enchanted mountains and crystal springs; one moment their hearts were filled with dread and the next with joy. She made the ocean move and forests grow and all who listened forgot that they stood in the courtyard of the king, for they had entered some enchanted place where the air was light with possibility.

When the daughter of the silversmith finished her story, they regarded her with awe, for as long as the gloom had touched their king and their kingdom, they had forgotten how to tell stories. Now that the story was over, they remembered where they were and once again they realized that there was no gift to hold, no gift to touch, no gift to take home to the palace. But they were no longer afraid. Instead, they looked up at their king, wondering.

The daughter of the silversmith stepped forward and said to the king, "Your majesty, tell us a story," and a hush fell over the people for he had never spoken to them except to give orders.

The king sighed a deep sigh and he looked into the face of each of his subjects as a storyteller looks at the listeners, and realizing that their hearts were open, he spoke.

"I WILL TELL you a story, although until this moment I did not know that I had a story to tell, nor a dance in my feet, nor a song in my voice. So forgive me if my words falter and forget how to find one another."

The people leaned forward, straining for each word, for they knew that what the king was going to say was not only his story but theirs.

THIS IS THE story the king told:

THERE WAS ONCE upon a time a sister and brother—prince and princess. The sister was first born and she had claim upon the crown. She was a beautiful girl who knew all there was to know of singing and dancing, and when the people saw her they rejoiced, for they knew that she would bring their lives joy and therefore prosperity.

But her brother was a jealous brother; he wanted to rule when he came of age, and he knew he would do better than she, for he cared about such things as treasure chests and land. She did not appreciate the power that would be hers. He did.

And because this young prince knew what power was, he said to his sister, "You don't really want to be queen over this great kingdom. Why, you'd have no time to dance and sing. Day and night you'd be worrying about people's troubles, staging wars, counting money. You wouldn't even have the time for dreams—for kings and queens do not sleep. My sister, let me be king and take this great burden from you."

"But my brother," she said, "perhaps I will be a different sort of ruler than all that."

Having tried persuasion, he resorted then to treachery, and one night he said, "My sister, come and dance with me tonight when the moon is high over the frozen silver lake." And that night the sky was so clear that the moon and lake were one and they danced on the frozen glass, round and round, until they reached the center, where he knew the ice was thin. When they came to that place he sent her twirling, the ice cracked, and she slipped beneath the frozen water.

The kingdom mourned the death of this beautiful princess, and when the mourning was over, they expected life to be as it had been. But when the prince became the king, a gloom settled over him. He won wars and he collected treasures from the corners of the wide land, but he never smiled. For though he had won the power he longed for, without the singing and dancing of his sister, he had no joy.

And every year on the longest day of the year he demanded

three gifts, gifts that had never been created before, and hope would rise in the king's heart, though he didn't know why. It was as if he waited for something, but when the gifts would come into his hands, he would touch them and hold them and take them back to the palace. Though they were fine, they did not satisfy his longing.

No one in the kingdom knew that the king had caused his sister's death, for ice holds no memory of footprints. But the king left a book with the story of his life to be read by his heir on the day he would take the crown. He bore only one son and on that day, a day that had always been one of rejoicing, the new king read the diary, and his heart too became heavy. And it was the same in the next generation. Thus the kingdom was wrapped in gloom that became darker and darker with time.

The king I have told you about was my grandfather, and each year, on the longest day of the year, I have waited for something, but I didn't know what it was. You have brought me many gifts in all the years I have been the king, and my palace is resplendent with their glitter and their fancy. But today you have brought me what I didn't know I wanted.

I thank you for what my grandfather did not know, and what my father never learned, and what I did not discover until now: That the gifts you can hold and touch and put on a shelf are not the same as the gifts that fill one's heart. The gifts of song and dance and story cannot break or splinter; they cannot call another jealous king to battle for they cannot be stolen or coveted, lost or protected. But once you have seen and listened, they cannot be forgotten. For the power of the song, the dance, and the story are greater by far than the power of a king."

Then the king spoke to the three women, the daughter of the goldsmith, the daughter of the jeweler, and the daughter of the silversmith:

"My grandfather wrote in his diary that we would suffer a long time but that one day his sister's spirit would return in forgiveness. My daughters, you have brought the gifts we have been waiting for, and now this gold crown weighs me down with all the sorrows of the past. Please come to me and lift this heavy crown from my head so that I may rule with a light and joyful heart."

They did so, and the gloom that had wrapped round that kingdom for a hundred and fifty years lifted and was gone.

The CRAFT *of* STORYTELLING

⋮

EVERY TEACHER can be a storyteller. It takes practice, but it is an attainable goal. Like the three daughters in *The Forgotten Gifts*, I believe that we all have enormous capacity for creativity. Unfortunately, we have come to believe that song, dance, and story belong to professional artists, not to us. We listen to their CD's, buy their books, and go to the movies while our own voices begin to grow rusty and our imaginations to grow dim. We receive these gifts passively, as the king does, accepting the interpretations of others rather than creating our own.

When we tell a story, we actively interpret the world. Stories connect us to the past and the future, to our families, friends, communities, and cultures. They describe us and define us. The stories we choose to tell are pictures of who we are.

Most teachers use storytelling informally and spontaneously. Something reminds us of a memory, and we share it. When I was a little girl, I would often come home from school, excited to retell the anecdote a teacher had shared about her dog, her mishap on the way to school, or her child. Most likely, my teacher did not realize that her moment of telling something of herself left a far greater impression on me than the math or reading lesson of the day.

The stories that teachers tell spontaneously are a wonderful part of any child's day, but after reading this book I hope that teachers will also consider using stories in a more conscious way that can ultimately influence both the behavior and the intellectual development of their students.

I HAVE BEEN teaching storytelling to teachers for many years at in-service workshops and at the Storytelling Arts annual weeklong institute for teachers. Through extensive interaction with teachers I have observed the easy transition from teaching to storytelling. The skills of teaching are remarkably similar to the skills of storytelling. Effective teachers, like storytellers, must have the presence to capture their students' attention and interest; speak with clarity; change tone and inflection to suit the situation; empathize with children's needs; improvise on the daily lesson; and have a clear sense for where they are going, how they are going to get there, and the flexibility to change course if necessary. Most teachers are both informal raconteurs and proficient readers of literature, the two related forms of story-making which help to hone a refined sense of language and story form.

Part of the desire to become a teacher stems from an impulse to share something we love with others. This, too, is the essence of storytelling. It is not just a love for story that makes a storyteller but a deep desire to transmit that story to someone else. A told story comes alive only during the telling, like the sleeping beauty who comes to life only when she is awakened by one who sees and loves her.

The story comes to life if and when we open ourselves to the many dimensions of the tale and our understanding of them. There is the doorway of feeling; the doorway of thought; the doorway of the body; the doorway of the visual imagination; and there is the doorway of the spirit where words cannot express our deep connections to the story world.

The most adaptable material for the teacher/storyteller is the folktale, and these are the tales that I will be referring to in the remainder of this book. These ancient stories speak about human nature in ways that are both profound and extremely accessible, capturing our deepest wishes and greatest fears, our silly mistakes and our clever schemes. A culture cannot transmit all of the personal stories that its people experience day to day, and folktales act as a shorthand version of our personal stories, capturing the essence of our life experiences. Some are wise and others are spooky, fanciful, comical or enchanting. Like poetry, they are metaphors for the obstacles, hopes, and dreams we encounter in our lives. They teach us about the sorts of characters we might encounter in life, and the choices and possibilities that may confront us. Many folktales translate well from one language and culture to another. We know that these stories have nomadic histories, since the same motifs appear in many parts of the world.

While folktales contain the story of our common humanity, they are, at the same time, stories that may reflect customs and beliefs of the culture from which they come. These tales hold a deep wisdom that has carried them across the river of time. They were originally told and not written, and many storytellers today depend upon texts of the folklorists and editors who have recorded and retold them. Despite the fact that these stories can now be found in books, they continue to be most powerfully transmitted through the spoken word.

I have learned an enormous amount about the structure

and pacing of dynamic storytelling through my own study and retelling of the folktale. Unlike modern literature, where the story often depends upon a character's internal change and development, the characters in folktales are endowed with distinct traits from the beginning that do not change but become fully realized through the characters' actions. The good and kind characters, for example, remain good and kind but may have to endure troubles in order to manifest their goodness in the world. The wicked and evil characters remain so throughout the tale, though in most cases their power is diminished in the end.

The folktale is structured simply, often with repetitive patterns, and folklorists have suggested that this helped traditional oral tellers to remember the stories. Likewise, those of us who continue to tell these stories can begin to internalize the structures of the tales while clothing them in a language that is natural to us. Although we need to be true to the tales, we can use our own language to tell them. It is important to realize that the telling is not a memorized word-for-word rendition of a text. The fact that folktales have no known author gives each teller the opportunity to look at different versions and create the tale anew through a personal sense of the characters, voices, dialogue, and images.

We must be all parts of the story to tell it; we must be the hero and the villain; we must live the life of the fairy and see the fairy world; and we must live the mundane and grim life of poverty. We must walk in the shoes of all the characters, see through their eyes, and experience their realities.

Understanding and empathy are the main tools of the storyteller. The storyteller knows the story in her heart and soul, and she conveys the nuance of emotion with subtlety and depth, not with artifice or melodrama. A story told well is a story that has been deeply lived and experienced by the teller, and even the most fanciful fairytale can be told first-hand if the teller has envisioned it with depth and clarity.

Any good story has a number of separate realities, and we must learn to move fluidly from one character to another. Unlike the actor who inhabits one character fully and completely, we must learn to touch our characters lightly and deeply at the same time, moving among them as a bee touches the petals of the flowers in a garden.

In this way we become the story and we live the story, but we cannot control it. Every telling must be different because we come to the world of the story anew each time we tell it. A writer's words take final form once they are published, but a storyteller's tale is never published. Every time we tell a story it lives a new life. When it is over, it continues to live inside the imaginations of those who hear it. In this way storytelling is an art form that defies the material world. Like the butterfly, it cannot be caught. Once caged, it will die.

IN WORKING with many teachers over the years, both in workshops and in their classrooms, I have come to understand the questions and objections they raise about using stories to teach. Before moving on to the ways storytelling affects the learning process of children, it is important to address these issues.

When I speak about storytelling to teachers, they often assume that I mean reading aloud. Although I am a staunch advocate of reading to children, it is important to realize that storytelling is an entirely different form of sharing stories. It does take more work to take a story within yourself and deliver it without a text, but the impact is well worth the effort.

There are several differences between storytelling and reading aloud that cause the children to react differently to them. When we read to children we are giving them a gift from another person, an author who has a good story to tell. The reader is the intermediary. But when we tell a story, the story is delivered as a gift directly from the self; it is as if we are unwrapping a precious package right before the child's eyes.

A reader of stories spends more time looking at the page than at the audience, while the storyteller is in constant contact with the audience and can make subtle adjustments to audience reactions. For example, we may use a gentler tone if we see fear cross a child's face, or we may explain a word if we observe a look of confusion.

Children who listen to a story are still and attentive. They are looking at the teller, but they are simultaneously seeing the images in their own imaginations. They are entranced. I believe that the compelling nature of the oral tale comes from the deep emotional connection of the teller to the story. This is relayed through our subtle nuances in tone and our continual eye contact.

Recently I told a story to a group of fifth grade students in Trenton and then asked them to write down what it felt like to listen. Most of them wrote that they felt as if they were "in the story." One girl compared it to reading when she wrote, "It feels better than reading the same story. It feels like the story came to life. Also there is a lot more emotion." Two children focused in on the empathetic relationships they felt as they listened. One wrote, "I feel amazing. As the person's telling the story you're imagining and picture it in your head. And you're replacing that character with yourself which makes it wonderful because you start to think, what if I was really in that position?" Another student wrote, "I feel like the story is really true. Like if a mother is suffering in the story you suffer too." Other students pointed out the accessibility of the material. One wrote, "It has more meaning than a story told from a book. It is calm and is very relaxable and I understand it better." And another said, "It has more life than a story told from a book, and everything makes it feel real."

A second grade teacher in Trenton shared a story with her class once a week. When she began to read a book to her class, a child asked, "Aren't you just going to tell with your mouth?" Another colleague told me that when she entered a second grade class a child called out, "She's the one who reads to us without a book."

Because we live in a highly literate society, we find it very difficult to put down the book and rely on our own language. We believe that the writers can say it better than we can. After being an avid reader all my life, I felt glued to the book when I started to tell stories. At first I thought I needed to memorize the language of the writer whom I perceived as the expert on language. I didn't trust my own language.

It took me quite a while to learn that my own language suited my own storytelling. Although I still believe that the writer's words may be far more artful than mine, written language is different from spoken. It is often more formal, and the writer cannot see the audience before his or her eyes as the storyteller can. We can be flexible with our language and adjust it to our audience.

Another hurdle we must jump in order to become storytellers is our own fear of performance, something widespread in our culture. Someone once told me that next to fear of death, one of the most prevalent fears in our culture is the fear of speaking in front of a group.

Because I loved stories so much and wanted to share them, I forced myself to work through the shaky knees stage. In fact, for several years I was so nervous that I could not stand up while telling a story, but my love of stories caused me to persevere.

A few years after I began telling stories, I was about to do a public performance where I had attended college, and there was some publicity in the newspaper. One evening I got a phone call from my freshman year Chinese professor who said that he had read about me in the paper. "I just wanted to know," he said, "whether you are the same Susan Danoff who was in my Chinese class." When I replied in the affirmative he said, "You were so shy, I just couldn't believe it was the same person."

A fifth grade teacher who took my storytelling institute after many years of teaching felt a similar performance anxiety. She said, "I was one of the shy ones. In fact, I practiced on the switchboard. I became a switchboard operator in college just to get myself so that I would have enough courage to stand up in a class. Because I wanted to teach. I knew I wanted to teach, but I didn't like the idea of standing up there and having everyone look at me, but now, man! I turn into this storyteller, and I can do this, and I'm funny! You know, it's a hoot! I really love it."

In teaching children to tell stories I have also discovered

that some of the quieter and more introspective children surprise their teachers with their ability to express themselves through story. One teacher said, "I have several kids in the class whose record cards had been noted as 'extremely shy, does not want to participate, very difficult to get to participate.' These have become some of my best storytellers, and I think it's because when they become storytellers they are not themselves any more. They become someone else, and this other person isn't shy."

Even if you're feeling shy or reticent to tell stories, I encourage you to try it. You will surprise yourself and your students, and gradually you will gain greater confidence. If there is a story you really love, you will find that the story itself will help you overcome your performance anxiety. In turn, you will be able to model this skill for your students, and they will surprise you and themselves.

Teachers also wonder how they can possibly fit storytelling into their day when there are so many other demands on their time. Keeping in touch with the teachers who have attended the Storytelling Arts weeklong summer institute over the past five years has helped me to discover the many ways that teachers are incorporating storytelling into their curriculum. They have told me that they use storytelling to teach writing, math, English as a Second Language, story structure, and vocabulary. Once they begin to use storytelling, they see that it is not just an extra thing to do but an engaging way to teach the skills they are already teaching.

In a second grade class in Elizabeth, NJ, one teacher uses stories in a bilingual (Spanish/English) language arts class in order to help her students understand the stories in their reading book. First they read the story together in the book, then she tells the story, and finally the children take the teacher's place and tell the story in their own words. This process allows the children to inhabit the language of the story. The second language begins to take on new life and meaning for them in the process.

A second grade teacher in Trenton uses storytelling to teach story elements. Since her students are struggling readers, she finds that by telling them a story she can teach them literary concepts. "Storytelling makes it so much easier for them to discuss questions such as who are the characters, what is the setting, what is the problem, and that sort of thing," she says, "because they don't have to struggle reading the words."

A fifth grade teacher in Mt. Olive has found numerous ways to incorporate storytelling into her writing curriculum. "It's seamless," she says, " and it supports so many of the skills that we're developing with the children. Fifth graders do so much writing. We get the organization, we get the character development, we get the dialogue. Their writing is so much more lively and so much more organized because they realize that if they are writing a story, it should be a jolly good story that somebody wants to read or listen to."

In schools where there is more than one teacher/storyteller, I have seen the teachers pool their resources, visiting one another's classes. That way, even a small repertoire can go a long way. In another school, the fifth graders tell stories to the first through fourth grades. Part of their challenge is finding appropriate material for their audience. Real audience is readily available in schools, and older children serve as models for younger children.

In Passaic the second grade teachers have their children perform group stories for the Latino festival. In Hamilton the principal starts her year by telling a story to all the children. In Roselle the fourth grade teacher uses narrative to teach math. A high school teacher for behaviorally disordered children is teaching storytelling skills to help raise the students' self esteem. Many of the preschool teachers we have worked with use storytelling on a regular basis to teach listening skills and language acquisition. Even preschool children can repeat entire stories, thus showing their mastery of vocabulary, sequencing, and dialogue.

In Mary Poppins' language, storytelling is "the spoon full of sugar that helps the medicine go down." The learning is fun and full of joy, but all the same, it's still learning. In the following chapters I will be providing many more examples—both from my own experience and from the experiences of other teachers—of how storytelling can be incorporated into the teaching of writing, reading comprehension, and emergent literacy.

You don't need to be a professional storyteller to tell stories, but you do need practice and guidance. Taking a workshop and joining a storytelling swap group can give you the tools you need. Try out new stories on your own children and your class. Involve them in the creating and retelling of stories. Read stories. As we work with our stories, we discover more about ourselves in the process, deepening our understanding, and delivering them to our audiences with more power.

For a parent or teacher, our audiences are always ready and waiting. We do not have to reach perfection before we tell them our stories. They can easily listen to us at any stage, and they will enjoy hearing our stories again and again. Some children don't like us to change a word after they latch on to a first telling, but they too must learn that every telling will be different. Even theirs, for they can learn to tell the stories back to us.

It takes time to develop a repertoire, and teaching is a demanding profession. Marie Shedlock suggested in her classic work *The Art of the Story-Teller* that teachers learn just a few stories slowly over time:

> *I realize the extreme difficulty teachers have to devote the necessary time to perfecting the stories they tell in school, because this is only one of the subjects they have to teach in an already overcrowded curriculum. To them I would offer this practical advice: Do not be afraid to repeat your stories. If you did not undertake more than seven stories a year, chosen with infinite care, and if you repeated these stories six times during the year of forty-two weeks, you would be able to do artistic, and therefore, lasting work; you would give a very great deal of pleasure to the children who delight in hearing a story many times. You would also be able to avoid the direct moral application, for each time a child hears a story artistically told, a little more of the meaning underlying the simple story will come to him without any explanation on your part.*

Fortunately, the children will request the same story over and over again, so that knowing one story does not necessarily mean that you will tell the story only once. Building a storytelling repertoire cannot be rushed, for what goes into your invisible story bag must be stories that speak so strongly to you that they become part of you. Let the bag fill slowly, over time, only with jewels, and they will be indestructible.

⁛

PART II

⁛

STORYTELLING *and* CLASSROOM CULTURE

The
TIGER'S
WHISKER
A Korean Folktale

THERE WAS ONCE a young woman named Yun Ok who had a problem. Her problem was as clear to her as the moon on a cloudless night. Yet the solution to her problem also seemed to her as distant as the moon itself.

ONE DAY she heard of a wise hermit who lived in the mountains. It was said that he made potions. Yun Ok went in search of him, and at last she found a man seated beneath a tree. He was an old man, old enough to be her grandfather, and something about his gaze made her guess that he was the wise man she sought.

"Excuse me, sir," she said. "My name is Yun Ok, and I have a problem. Are you the wise man I have heard of? The man who makes potions? I have a little money in my pocket, and I can pay you if you could please make me a potion."

The man said nothing for a while. He merely gazed at her. She began to grow uncomfortable, when at last he spoke.

"So, they're saying in the village that I make potions, are they? Potions to heal a sore throat? Yes, I can do that. These woods have many secrets that I know. Potions to help a woman bear a child? Perhaps. Potions to bring rain? No. No one can do that. I know these woods well, child, but if they have made you believe that potions are magic, I cannot help you. Never mind. I talk too much. Tell me, what is this problem you have that can be cured by a potion?"

"It is my husband. Three years ago he went off to fight in a war. Since he has come back, he is not at all the same as he used to be. He used to be gentle, and now he speaks harshly to me. When I place food before him, he pushes it away. Sometimes when he's working in the fields, he stares off in the distance and does nothing. And he hardly looks at me, at least not the way he used to."

"Yes," said the wise man. "Sometimes it is that way with men who come back from a war. But still, you have not answered my question. What sort of potion is it that you seek?"

"I need a potion that will make my husband the way he used to be."

"Ah," said the wise man. "It is that kind of potion you want." He thought for a few minutes and then he said, "I will think about your potion. Come back in three days."

THREE DAYS later Yun Ok ran all the way back to the mountain. She found the wise man sitting beneath the same tree.

"Do you have it?" she asked breathlessly. "Do you have my potion?"

"I have thought a great deal about this potion that you need," he said, "and it requires one essential ingredient, and only you may get it for me. Bring me the whisker of a living tiger, and you shall have your potion."

"What? The whisker of a living tiger? But how can I do that?"

The mountain hermit refused to say anything more, and Yun Ok walked home slowly.

IT WAS KNOWN to Yun Ok and all the other villagers that a tiger lived nearby. They had learned to keep out of the tiger's way, and the tiger kept out of their way. But that night, when her husband was asleep, Yun Ok got out of bed and went near the cave where the tiger was reputed to live. She could not see the tiger, but she thought he might be there, and she spoke to him.

"Tiger. My name is Yun Ok. I have a problem, and you're the only being in the world who can help me. I mean no harm. Every night I am going to come and visit you." Yun Ok talked to him a while longer, sang him a song, and went home.

She did this the next night and the next night and every night for a whole month.

At the beginning of the second month she went closer to the place where the tiger lived. She saw him at last, for the moonlight was caught in his eyes.

"Tiger," she said, "it's me, Yun Ok. You can see that I

don't have any weapons. I mean no harm." And she spoke to him for a while longer, sang him a song, and went home.

She did this the next night and the next night and every night for a whole month.

At the beginning of the third month Yun Ok took a large wooden bowl and filled it with leftovers from her dinner.

"Tiger. I've brought you a little present. I hope you like my cooking."

She placed the bowl on the ground near the tiger, moved back, and watched him eat. She did this the next night and the next night and every night for a whole month.

At the beginning of the fourth month, Yun Ok held the bowl of food in her two hands. "Come, my friend," she said. "Come and eat from the bowl in my hands."

The tiger came, and as he ate she could see his great tongue lapping up the food and his great teeth chewing it. But he did not harm her.

She did this the next night and the next night and every night for a whole month.

At the beginning of the fifth month, after the tiger had finished eating she said, "My friend, your fur looks so soft. I am going to pet you." She stroked the tiger between his ears, and he purred.

She did this the next night and the next night and every night for a whole month.

At the beginning of the sixth month Yun Ok said, "My friend, for five months I have been coming to see you. I have talked to you. I have sung to you. I have brought you food. I have petted you. And now....I need something from you. I need one of your whiskers. I promise, it won't hurt at all."

And quickly, she clipped one of his whiskers, and he didn't mind at all.

THE NEXT DAY she hurried off to find the mountain hermit, the whisker clutched in her small hand. It was winter, and this time she found him sitting in his small hut in front of a fire.

"I have it!" she said. "I have the tiger's whisker!"

The hermit took it from her and examined it carefully.

"How did you get this whisker?" he asked.

"For a whole month I went to the place where the tiger lived, and though I couldn't see him, I spoke with him and sang to him. The next month I went closer and closer until I could actually see him, and I sang to him some more. The third month I brought him food and placed it before him. The fourth month I actually held the bowl in my own hands, and he ate from it. The fifth month, after he ate, I petted him. And just yesterday, I clipped his whisker, and there you have it. So now I have brought you the ingredient you need for my potion."

"I see," said the mountain hermit.

Then he took the whisker and threw it into the fire.

"What have you done?" cried Yun Ok. "For five whole months I have worked to get that whisker for the potion, and now you have destroyed it."

"Tell me," said the wise man, "which is more ferocious: a tiger or your husband? You do not need the whisker. You already have the potion."

THAT NIGHT THERE was a full moon in the sky, and it seemed so close, Yun Ok felt she could almost touch it.

ONCE UPON A TIME
Storytelling as Preparation for Learning

∙∴∙

S EVERAL YEARS ago Storytelling Arts was working in a preschool in Elizabeth, New Jersey. A substitute in the kindergarten class was having so much difficulty with her students that the principal asked the pre-k teacher to take the children for the rest of the day. Several of the children with severe behavior problems were on the waiting list to be tested for learning disabilities. Just then, storyteller Jim Rohe was scheduled to arrive in the pre-k class. The teacher said to the principal, "Please stay for a few minutes and see what happens when the storyteller comes."

What the principal saw was that all of the children, including those who had been giving the substitute the hardest time, immediately calmed down and listened to the stories. At the end of the class the teacher said to the principal, "We don't need more special education teachers in this school; we just need more storytelling."

For years I have been experiencing similar responses from teachers. They tell us that their most challenging students can sit for stories. Children who are labeled "communications handicapped" have astonished their teachers when they recall the details of a story even more accurately than their classmates. Grants to schools for behaviorally disordered children have shown us that even children who have the most difficulty attending and getting along with their peers can listen attentively to stories, respond to them, and retell them.

Teenage boys in detention, many of whom have learning disabilities in addition to criminal records, listen too. Their tough exteriors sometimes seem to vanish as they listen, and at the end of the story they are eager to share their thoughts and feelings. The first time my colleague Joanne Epply-Schmidt and I told stories at Mercer County Detention Center, the boys talked with us for over an hour, and when we left they asked us when we were returning. The assistant superintendent said, "I can hardly believe what I just saw. We have so much difficulty getting these boys to open up. I've never seen them engage in a discussion like this." Since that time we've been visiting the facility on a weekly basis.

Every teacher has to deal with tough issues of classroom management. As I mentioned in the introduction, I quit my first teaching job because of behavior problems. I've thought a great deal about why stories break through to children, but it was not until I attended an educational sociology course with Terry O'Conner at The College of New Jersey that I found a way to explain why storytelling has such a powerful impact on teacher/student relationships and group dynamics.

THE RELATIONSHIP between teacher and students is sometimes like the one between Yun Ok and the tiger in *The Tiger's Whisker*, especially at the beginning of the school year when they are total strangers. The children don't know the teacher, her rules, her style, her expectations, her classroom management style, or the skills they are to master. Sometimes they don't even know one another. There is a significant period of adjustment which teachers and children must experience before learning can even take place. Add to this, the great diversity in American culture and the fact that some children do not even speak the same language as the teacher, and we can begin to empathize with feelings of fear, distrust, anxiety, and discomfort that some children bring with them to school.

Yet our schools are so set on what children must learn, we often forget that if they are not prepared to learn, the fruits of the teaching will be greatly diminished. The importance of the time a teacher takes to familiarize the children with her expectations and the community of learners is essential to the children's subsequent learning. Like Yun Ok's gentle and gradual approach to the tiger, it can take a significant amount of time to establish a meaningful relationship.

Sociologists tell us that each classroom is a culture unto itself, a discourse community with its "discourse practices," the language, actions, and behaviors acceptable within that culture. Students walking through the door on the first day of school may have heard stories about their new teacher that may be truths, half-truths, or falsehoods. They must be prepared to learn the new rules, gauge what is important to the teacher, establish which skills they should already know and which they are expected to learn, and get to know the others in the community.

Some of the most common classroom discourse practices involve the way the teacher expects the students to interact with her and one another. In some classrooms students are expected to be quiet unless spoken to, to raise their hands if they wish to speak, and to talk with the teacher and not with other children. Some classrooms allow children to work collaboratively and help one another on problems, while in others this is considered cheating. Some traditional classrooms have the chairs neatly in rows with all students facing the teacher, while others have children's desks clustered together so that they may work in groups. In some classrooms, all the children work on the same task at the same time, while in others, students separate into a variety of work areas. Some teachers require absolute silence at all times while others tolerate quiet interactions.

Sociologists believe that some students who cannot understand, relate to, or master the discourse practices in a classroom may be perceived as troublemakers. Other children may be determined to make themselves as invisible as possible, trying not to speak or be spoken to, in order to avoid mistakes or failure. The "good" students who master the practices can operate comfortably and easily.

Entering this new community, a student must also be prepared to accept the discourse practices and feel safe. Is the teacher strict or lenient? Is she understanding or rigid? The student worries, "Am I safe to express myself or must I be careful what I say? Am I safe from ridicule from the teacher and other children?" Although most students are safe from physical harm within the borders of classroom culture, the fear for one's emotional safety can be very great.

Sociologists have determined that children cannot succeed without establishing "trusting relationships" with their teachers. When students are uncomfortable with the discourse practices in the classroom, either because they don't understand them or because the practices are significantly different than the other cultures the students are familiar with, their learning is severely impeded. According to sociologist Raymond P. McDermott, "Anecdotal reports of children learning to read suggest that the successful acquisition of literacy ...depends on the achievement of trusting relations. Many of our children spend most of their time in relationship battles rather than on learning tasks. This is especially true for minority children who enter the schools with an uncertain status in the eyes of teachers."

Considering that a student must understand the classroom discourse and feel a sense of trust with the teacher and community, teachers cannot begin to teach content before they have established a working community. By investing time in creating a classroom culture of trust and understanding, the students will be prepared to learn. When teachers make the discourse practices clear to the students and even involve them in the creation of practices, students can take ownership of the culture and develop what sociologists call "solidarity," or commitment to the culture.

STORYTELLING IS itself a form of classroom discourse that can have profound impact on the trusting relationships between children and their teachers. The teacher who takes on the role of storyteller creates an atmosphere of welcome, non-judgemental interaction, and emotional safety for children that can resonate throughout the school day and year.

Imagine that the students and their teacher sit in a circle for a story, for a circle has neither top nor bottom, beginning nor end. Everyone takes an equal role of importance and can see everyone else. When the teller begins, "Once upon a time," the walls of the classroom recede like magic, and all the children enter another time and place along with the teacher. Sometimes children may take part in the story, joining in chants, songs, and repetitive dialogue. At other times the story may become so enchanting that the story-teller's voice drops to a whisper; no one misses even the sound of a bee's wing touching the petal of a flower.

When we share a story, it must come not just from our memory or intellect, but from the heart. We must identify with the emotions of the characters, allowing the listeners to become enraptured with the drama that the characters face. For a very young child, anticipating what Baby Bear will feel when he sees that his porridge is all eaten up or his chair is broken, is high drama indeed.

The sharing of a story is a gift of immeasurable value from the teacher to the child, because the children realize the authenticity of the gift even if they cannot name it. They instinctively feel that as the teacher gives the story to them, she is giving them something from her heart, something they recognize as love.

This gift provides a stark contrast to other discourse practices. Sociologists have determined that the majority of a teacher's time is spent using a strategy called I.R.E. (teacher Inquires, students Responds, teacher Evaluates). In this frequent verbal interaction with students, teachers are testing to see whether students have retained specific information. Unlike authentic conversation where we ask questions in order to discover something, the teacher requests answers she already knows. Although open–ended questions can stimulate thoughtful discussion, the I.R.E. involves close-ended questions with only one correct response. Fear of judgment, of failure to produce the right answer, and of disappointing the teacher can hinder a child's desire to respond.

Strategies to maintain order in a classroom also cause a teacher to use directive language with children. Students are often told what they can and cannot do, since rules are necessary to avoid chaos in the classroom. Providing information, testing for correctness, and giving orders are three of the most common ways teachers speak with children.

The story voice provides a distinct contrast to many of these modes of interaction. The language of story is a language that children and teacher share as equals. Story is a language of inclusion, not of judgment. It is also a language of intimacy. To tell a story well, you must share something you care about. Doing so reveals the emotion and spirit of the teller. Children have special radar for authentic expression of self, and they know when an adult is speaking to them honestly, openly, and compassionately. Storytelling in the classroom gives teachers the opportunity to invite children through the door of the inner self. By knowing their teacher in this way, children are more apt to let the teacher know them. This can become the basis for a trusting relationship.

My colleague Tara McGowan taught storytelling to fifth grade students while she was doing her student teaching, and she wrote, "When I was telling a story, my students focused their attention on me more consistently than at any other time. As one student put it, I was more 'me' when I was teaching storytelling than when I was teaching other subjects where I took a more conventional approach." She captured the essence of the trusting relationship when she reflected, "The self-confidence I have observed in my students and felt in myself through learning storytelling techniques, happens because our empathy and self-knowledge is tapped and validated in ways we do not often experience in the classroom.

Clearly, empathy and self-knowledge are as important in the teacher as they are in the student, and through storytelling I was able to model this for my students."

After teaching for many years, fourth grade teacher Diane Jannuzzelli felt much like Tara in terms of her relationship with the students. She wrote, "I feel that the students' perception of me is different when I'm telling a story. These [storytelling] workshops have enabled me to come out of myself and that has enhanced my teaching."

When I first began to share stories with young children, I was both surprised and gratified at their responses when I entered or left the room. I was often greeted affectionately, and sometimes, being a small person, I could barely stand up as the children offered great group hugs before I left. They were saying thank you in their way and loving me back for offering them what they perceived as a gift of love. I also noticed that if I returned to a school where I had visited before, children would stop me in the halls and say, "Didn't you tell me a story?" I was touched by the fact that they used the word "me" and not "us," indicating that the experience was a deeply personal one. When I was doing a lot of work in New Jersey schools, children would sometimes approach me in public places and introduce me to their parents as "my storyteller."

WHEN WE teach, we offer information as we tell children what they need to do, but the subject matter is frequently devoid of emotional content. Stories are, by contrast, filled with emotion that speaks directly to children. I have often wondered why children listen so raptly to stories, and I have come to believe that stories speak directly to their emotional needs.

Stories also provide a safe place to experience emotions. It may be scary when the Gunniwolf is following Little Daughter or when the troll is waiting for the Billy Goats Gruff under the bridge, but the children know that the storyteller will ultimately keep them safe. Emotions form the inner fabric of a story, and they change moment to moment. We can experience fear or longing, wishing or despair, but the storyteller will also take us through the necessary transformations of emotional experience that prove to us that a single emotion is never frozen in time. Little Daughter may be momentarily frightened by the Gunniwolf, but children know that she will outwit him and find safety in the end just as they know that the Billy Goats Gruff will all make it to the other side of the bridge.

For children who experience a great deal of trauma at home and in their communities, stories are also a nonthreatening way to revisit emotions. It's true, at home they may not always be okay, but stories are a source of hope and possibility. The Cinderella character that is present in hundreds of folktales around the world may represent the part of ourselves that faces cruelty and deprivation but somehow finds a way to transcend it. Or the third son who is called the fool or the simpleton, triumphs to show the rest of the community that they have misperceived him all along.

Listening to the teacher/teller, children relax in a deep place within themselves which allows, for the moment, freedom from anxiety and expectations, their own and others. Teenagers in the Mercer County Youth Detention Center consistently comment that stories "free their minds" and help them relax. These young people, who live in an almost constant state of tension, come through the door of imagination effortlessly and willingly. Storytellers see this in classrooms everywhere, whether young people are troubled or not.

One of the most surprising findings in the data we have collected from teachers in Storytelling Arts classrooms is that children who are usually shy or reticent to speak will participate during storytelling. A preschool teacher in East Orange wrote, "We had one little girl who would never participate. She whispered her name for the first time when the storyteller came." I have come to believe that these children are most fearful and distrustful of the ordinary classroom discourse practices. Storytelling is a form of discourse that helps them feel comfortable and confident.

I was one of those children. When I began kindergarten in the late 1950's, I attended schools that were extremely old-fashioned and strict. Our chairs were in rows, we weren't allowed to whisper to a friend, and we could never ask for help from anyone but the teacher. The term "collaborative learning" had not yet been thought of in my part of the world. Most of what we were asked to learn was rote memorization. Although I did well in school, I was always afraid that I would say the wrong answer and be reprimanded, even though I hardly ever was. I thought that the quieter I was, the more likely the teacher wouldn't notice me. I never had a storytelling teacher, but I have tried to become the teacher I never had.

The powerful emotional fabric of the story and its ability to bond teacher and children can provide the foundation for the trusting relationships that lies at the heart of a child's willingness to learn. The language of story is unlike the language that teachers may use at other times of the day. It is not the language of instruction, judgment, command, reprimand, order, explanation, questioning, testing, or information. It is an emotionally charged language that provides entry into worlds of enchantment and transformation. When children hear their teacher speak this language, they have the feeling that the teacher cares about them, knows them, and understands them.

Folktales are no less powerful today than they always were. In fact, sometimes as I watch children listen to stories, they remind me of parched plants that have been waiting for water. Listening to a story told simply and directly by another human being is an intensely personal experience, entirely different from a "made for everyone" movie or TV show. Even after one classroom visit, I have noticed that children are not afraid to look me in the eyes; they wave and say hello in the halls as if we have been friends for a long time. Listening children sometimes hold onto the story, the relationship with the teller, or a personal moment of truth.

And perhaps, if we're lucky, even the tiger can be tamed.

MAKING STONE SOUP:
Storytelling in Community

∴

ONCE SHE has begun to build trusting relationships with individual children, a successful teacher must also create a positive dynamic for the community of learners and develop "solidarity." Storytelling offers teachers a method for providing authentic shared experiences that helps to bond members of the community.

Storytelling is an act of friendship. The story itself is like an invisible thread, connecting teller and listener(s). As a storyteller shares a tale with a group, that invisible thread is like a spider's web, connecting all of the listeners and the teller. The ability to connect is the foundation for friendship. The teacher who tells stories demonstrates this fundamental element of friendship, creating a community of caring.

At the beginning of the school year, the members of a class remind me of the well-known folktale *Stone Soup*. A hungry traveler comes into a village of people who are not eager to share their food with a stranger. He tells them that he can make soup from a stone if they will provide just a pot and some water. One woman willingly does so, and he plops his stone in. Then he suggests that perhaps the soup will taste a little better with a potato, and someone fetches one. After that he adds, "Perhaps a soup bone might enhance the flavor," and someone else gets one. This goes on for some time as various people bring vegetables, meat, and salt. At the end of the evening, the whole village shares soup with the stranger as they marvel that the stranger could have made such a soup from "just a stone."

A class of children is not unlike stone soup in its composition, resembling a hodgepodge of ingredients, not always harmonious. It takes a concerted effort to bring the children together, to focus their attention and energy, and to help them look at one another, not as strangers, but as friends. The story, plopped like a stone in the middle of such a group, can be the magic ingredient that we need to bring the disparate elements into harmony.

When we talk about social consciousness, we are really referring to the awareness that we carry of ourselves and others. Young children carry very little of this awareness, and school is often the first place where they must cope with a community of people who must share the same resources: teacher, toys, and food. Every mother and preschool teacher knows how much time must be spent in helping children learn to share. The first word my son learned when he attended home daycare at one year old was "mine's." In supervising the play of young children, helping children to share and take turns is the role of vigilante moms and daycare providers. As children grow older, they may not grab things from one another in quite so blatant a manner, but the jealousies may continue in new forms. Sometimes older children and adults also want what others have, but they learn to vie for power and use manipulative strategies to get it.

Story is something without material form, making it possible for any number of people to share it at the same time. As the children gather to listen, the story is something that belongs to every member of the circle simultaneously.

Paradoxically, it is also an individual gift, as each receiver takes it in and makes of it what he/she will. In a culture which instills in children an insatiable desire for material things, the story momentarily detaches us from tangible reality and puts us in touch with what is deeply felt. The story exists only in imagination, and when the storyteller has finished telling it, it belongs entirely to each and every listener.

As children attend to the teacher/teller, they learn an important social skill—the skill of listening—and they learn it in a way that comes naturally. Listening is easy when you want to hear what is being said, and even those children who are not considered good listeners usually excel at story listening. There is an intangible element of good storytelling that is simply disarming. Listening children temporarily forget where they are, they drop the armoring that they may wear the rest of the day, and they enter the world of the story. The storyteller models this behavior as she completely enters the world of the story, sweeping everyone up into believing. This partially explains the universal comment by teachers who tell us that their most challenging students behave appropriately during storytelling time.

To be effective in any form of social relations, we must learn to be good listeners. One of the reasons that a story is almost irresistibly compelling to a listener has to do with its emotional content. We become engaged in the characters' emotions and want to follow their progress towards resolution. We are not satisfied until we know how things will turn out, and we wish to follow the characters to a state of safety and contentment.

Listening to a told story is both a private and public act, simultaneously connecting us more deeply to self and to others. Story time resembles an almost enchanted moment where the self seems to dissolve, allowing room for story beings to enter consciousness. We become so caught up in the imagined world, we momentarily forget the material world.

In those moments when we are emotionally connected to the story world, we learn a second social skill essential to community consciousness: we learn to identify with others. Awareness of others' conflicts, pain, hardships, and triumphs can inform a child's future understanding of self and others. It is the critical ingredient necessary for empathy.

Reading also creates many opportunities for learning empathy, but there are many school children who either cannot or do not choose to read. For these children, story-telling can be a door to the complexities of human feeling that help us to validate our own experiences and create bridges to others.

Stories are compact metaphors, and when we hear them, it is as if we hold a mirror up to an inner self, a self that we cannot ordinarily see, especially in school. The folktale in particular carries an elemental sense of life's struggles, stripped of ornamentation. Our wishes, hopes, fears, and desires are exposed in these tales where goodness triumphs and wisdom reveals the folly of greed and cruelty. The neglected daughter rises above her hardship; the aged couple longs for a child to keep them company; the third brother who is considered a fool outsmarts everyone; the abused sister becomes the queen. People all over the world have told these stories in order to find a reason to keep living, the courage to overcome obstacles, the faith in human kindness and generosity.

Just as the experience of listening to a story may help

children to develop empathy, having the opportunities to discuss the ideas in stories can help them to put names to feelings and consciously articulate ideas. My colleagues in Storytelling Arts and I have often noticed that students have no trouble listening to the teacher/storyteller but may struggle to give the same respectful attention to their classmates. We see that children are so hungry to be recognized and have their own ideas validated that some do not have the patience and attention to listen to other children.

If children are to create a successful community, they need to be heard and to listen to others. Like any skill worth practicing, this doesn't come easily for some children, but it is not an impossible feat. As the students are encouraged to engage in questions that challenge them to think and to share their ideas with their classmates, real conversation can begin in the classroom, conversation that allows them to hear one another and express themselves. In this way their social consciousness grows by beginning with the community closest to home.

Teachers must remember that even if a story seems simple, it depicts a multidimensional world that resonates differently with each listener. Sometimes it is enough just to share a story and ask no questions, allowing children to privately meditate on the meaning of the story. Some teachers ask children to share whatever they wish at the conclusion of the telling. If we do choose to ask questions, it is vital to ask the open-ended questions that will not cut off a student's personal relationship to the tale. "What is the meaning or moral of the story?" is not a helpful question, for it suggests that there is one "right" answer and closes down the possibility for many meanings. Instead the question, "What does the story mean *to you?*" opens up to the child what he or she already knows: that within the story resides a meaning for him or her alone, one that may comfortably be shared or not, but one that is nonetheless present.

In being asked to share their thoughts freely and without judgment, children have the ability to be heard. This validation and simple appreciation is a gift to young learners. They are given an opportunity to converse freely without the judgment of being right or wrong. Stories, like prisms, throw light in so many directions, one never knows where an illuminating insight may reside.

As the classroom struggles to achieve solidarity, the story circle also offers the opportunity for authentic group experience. The children live the drama of *Jack and the Beanstalk* as they listen and then move on to tend their growing plants with extra special care, paying special attention to how fast or big they might grow, and wondering, if they hold treasure, what it might be. Or they hold a stone and remember the American Indian story of the storytelling stone that once shared all the stories in the world with a young orphan boy.

Storytelling Arts research in preschool classrooms has shown that children play act stories during their free time on the playground, the sandbox, or the dress up areas. Even at the Detention Center, teenagers retell stories they have heard months before. In this way the stories become a common language and reference point for all of the students who have heard, shared, and experienced them.

Since the stories we often share orally are international folktales, they may also help bridge gaps for children who are uncomfortable with some of the classroom discourse practices but who share stories in their home culture. Many years ago I told a Mexican story to a second grade class where there was only one Spanish-speaking child. The story required that we count to ten in Spanish several times, and this child was able to lead the group. Some days later I received a crumpled up love note from that child whose self-esteem had risen substantially that day when his own culture had been acknowledged in a positive way.

In classrooms where cultural diversity may create misunderstandings and distrust, sharing international folktales can help children take pride in their own cultures while learning to respect the culture of others. Even a young child who has heard and enjoyed a story from a faraway place, may some day meet a person from that country, remember the story, and feel a human connection. Students may also be encouraged to tell stories they have heard from their home cultures, thus deepening their own and their classmates' appreciation of that culture. Visiting parents who come to share stories from their native lands can also strengthen the classroom community. Still, the teacher's example remains foremost in creating an accepting environment for stories through her own telling and appreciation of students' tales from home.

Inevitably there are struggles within any classroom, and sometimes a story may help the class to understand and reflect upon the existing conflicts. In Waldorf School classrooms where storytelling is used for both instructional and behavioral reasons, teachers are encouraged to tell stories that mirror a problem they may see without calling direct attention to it. In Native American culture, elders share stories with misbehaving children in place of punishment to help influence behavior in a gentle, memorable, and persuasive manner.

Classroom teachers can find ways to select stories that have metaphoric relationships to troubling issues, though it is important to do so subtly, without calling attention to the behavior of a particular child or children. In this way, stories become gifts to grow on.

When my son was very young, he would ask me whether I knew people whom we would pass on the street. His world was defined solely by his own concrete reality. For children, social consciousness develops over a long period of time, beginning at home and school. The borders of a child's world gradually expand, as he/she recognizes that there are numerous people in the world, languages he/she will never understand, books too numerous to count, distances too great to fathom, creatures and landscapes far different from those outside the school yard. In a gentle way, as the stories they hear begin to build bonds within the class community, the stories also connect children to the vast world beyond the borders of the classroom, teaching them that the ability to relate to others begins in the heart.

PART III

STORYTELLING *and* IMAGINATION

The LOST CHILD

A Scottish Folktale

A long time ago in a faraway place near the sea, there once lived a young woman who had nothing at all in the world, except a baby. Her parents had died and her husband was gone too. Yet she loved this baby so very much that rather than thinking of herself as the very poorest person in all the world, which she surely was, she thought herself the richest.

She wandered from town to town, the baby in her arms or strapped to her back, looking for work. Somehow she managed to find a bit of work here and there, food enough to fill their stomachs, and shelter on cold nights.

One afternoon she needed to climb down to the river to get some water. Carefully she wrapped her baby in her red plaid shawl and placed him in a mossy spot under a tree. As she climbed down the rocks to the water, her foot slipped, and she tumbled down to the rocks below.

Later that day two fisherman noticed what looked like a human form upon the rocks. They were able to sail their boat in, and they found her, unconscious but alive. They took her home to their womenfolk and asked them to tend to her, and they laid her down near the fire.

That night she opened her eyes, and when she found herself staring into the faces of strangers, she did not ask, "Who are you?" Instead she said, "Where is my baby?"

When the women did not answer, she asked again, "Where is my baby?"

The women did not know what to say, for the fishermen had said nothing about a baby. At last one of them said, "The fishermen found you alone on the rocks. Perhaps when you fell, the baby flew from your arms into the water."

"Oh, no," she said, "that could not be. For I laid him down beneath a tree before I climbed down. Quick, please take me to the land above the place the fishermen found me, for my baby will be cold and scared and hungry."

"No," they said. "You must stay here and rest your injured bones. We will go and look."

When she insisted, they carried her to the place above the rocks, but when she looked at the mossy place beneath the tree, the baby was gone.

"Perhaps someone heard the baby cry and took him home," she said. "Let us go and knock on all the doors of the fisherfolk."

"You are too injured to do that," they said, "we will go."

And this time, she had to agree. The women did as she asked. They knocked on every door in the village asking for the baby, but no one had so much as heard the cry of a wee babe.

When the young woman was almost fully healed, she said to the fisherfolk, "I thank you for all you've done for me, but I must go in search of my baby, even if it means to the ends of the earth and beyond."

"Child, you are welcome to stay and be one of us," they said. "But you must do what you must do. If you find your baby and wish for a home, please return to us."

"That I will," she said, "for you have been more than father and mother to me."

Thanking them once more, she went on her way.

The first thing she did was to knock on every door in that village again, asking and asking yet again, "Have you found a baby? He was wrapped in a red plaid shawl. His eyes sparkle like the sea when the sun dances on the waves, and his hair is the color of corn silk."

She asked and she asked, but no one had seen the baby, and she walked from village to village. Her desire never weakened, but little by little her hope began to fade.

She had traveled a hundred days when she met a band of gypsies. Buoyed by the hope that these travelers might see what other people cannot, she inquired after her baby.

"The only babies we have are our own," they said. But hearing her story and seeing her despair they said, "Go with us. In a week's time we are meeting up with more of our kind. There is an old woman among them who is very wise. We say she knows all that time itself remembers. Perhaps she can help you."

The young woman traveled that week with the

gypsies, and at the week's end they met up with the others. They took her into a little hut where there was a fire burning, and there she beheld the most ancient face she had ever seen but with eyes as bright as a child's.

"Come," said the old woman when she had heard the story. "Come, and sit by my fire, and we shall see what we shall see."

All night long they sat and stared in the fire, until at last the last ember died. Then the old woman said, "I have seen where you baby has gone. The fairies of Sidh have stolen him."

"Then he is alive! And I shall get him back."

"True," said the old woman, "he is alive. But I fear no mortal could ever get him back."

"Then I will lay down right here and die," she said.

"Well, if you're willing to die for him then you may as well die trying. I can tell you a bit about the Sidh folk that may help you. They have powerful magic, it is true, but they have one weakness. They are unable to make anything for themselves. Whatever they have they must either beg or steal. And they love beautiful things. So if you want your baby back, perhaps you could trade something beautiful for him."

"But look at me," said the young woman. "I have nothing at all in the world. How could I get something precious?"

"I cannot help you. You shall find what you shall find."

"And where are the fairies?"

"Ah," said the old woman, "that I can tell you.

In a month's time all the Sidh fairies will gather in a secret place, and I can tell you how to find them."

"But how will I get into their secret meeting?"

"You must buy your way in.," said the old woman. "I can tell you no more. But I can say a blessing over you."

And circling her hand round the top of the young girl's head she said, "Protect her from fire and water, air and earth."

The young woman thanked the old one and went to sit by the sea to think. And as she watched the waves pounding the rocks, she realized that she would need not one gift, but two. One to buy her way into the secret meeting, and the other to buy her baby out.

And as she sat there, she no longer felt that she was the richest person in all the world but the poorest. She had nothing but her worn clothes, the plate and cup she carried in her satchel, a fork, a spoon, and a needle.

And all the bounty of nature itself.

As she looked at the natural world around her, suddenly her poverty vanished amidst the wonders of her imagination. She began to remember stories, and the two most beautiful objects she had ever heard tell of were the white cloak of Nechtan and the beautiful harp of Wrad.

Then she knew what she must do.

She began to climb down the rocks, gathering the down of the white ducks, and placing it in her bag. And as she worked, the rocks did not scar her feet, nor did the sun burn her or the wind keep her from her task, for the blessing of the gypsy woman was with her.

When she had gathered every bit of pure white down that she could find, she sat on the beach and began to weave a cloak. Then she cut off all her blond hair and put several pieces aside. Using the hair as thread, she embroidered pictures of golden flowers and birds all around the border of this full-length cloak. When she finished, it looked like a cloud that had been embroidered by the gods.

Then she walked up and down the beach, this time gathering white bones polished by the sea and sand and carried by the waves. She fashioned them into a harp, and with the golden hairs that she had saved, she strung her harp. When she finished and laid her fingers on the strings, the notes were so pure and filled with longing that the gulls hovered in the air to listen.

Now she had a week left to reach the secret meeting place of the Sidh fairies, and she traveled with the harp under one arm and the cloak over the other and the image of her baby held fast in her mind.

The night of the meeting, she stood among the bushes, watching the Sidh folk as they gathered. These were not the wee fairy folk but fairies the size of regular humans. When all had gathered except for one straggler, she laid out the cloak on the ground and stood in front of it.

When the fairy woman saw her, she said, "What are you doing here? Mortals are not allowed."

And then the young woman stepped back and the Sidh fairy saw the cloak. Her eyes were bedazzled and she forgot her anger.

"What will you take for this cloak?"

""There's only one in the world," she said, "and it's not for sale."

"I'll fill that bag of yours with gold."

"Gold is worth nothing to me. But it does have its price."

"Name it."

"Take me into the secret meeting with you, and you shall have it."

"All right. Now hand it over."

"Nay," said the young woman, knowing their thieving ways. "Take me in first, and then it shall be yours."

When they entered the fairy place, the other fairies were angry when they saw the mortal woman, but when their eyes fell upon the cloak, they forgot all about her and only wished to try it on.

Then she went to the center of the gathering where the king was seated on his throne, and she stood before him with her harp.

"What have you there, mortal?" he asked.

"A harp," she said.

"I have many such harp," he said.

"Perhaps," she said, "but not a one like this." And so saying, she plucked the strings, and the sound was so pure and filled with longing, that the fairy king felt there was nothing in the world he had ever wanted more.

Trying to conceal his desire, he said, "It's a nice harp. What will you take for it?"

"There's only one like it," she said, "and it's not for sale."

"Come now," he said, "I'll give you a silk cloak and fill the pockets with gold."

"No," she said, "It's not for sale."

"I'll give you a jeweled ring for all ten of your fingers."

"No," she said, "It's not for sale."

"Name your price," he said, "Whatever you ask you shall have."

And this was just what she had been waiting for.

"Give me my baby, and you shall have the harp."

The king was stunned, for he did not know until that moment that she was the mother of the beautiful mortal babe. But now he'd trapped himself in his own net and could not withdraw the words he had spoken.

Then at his command, his servants began to pile up jewels upon jewels around her feet until they reached her knees. "Here," he said, "these jewels are yours in exchange for the harp."

"No," she said, "I want the baby." And she thought that the sparkle in her baby's eyes was far more beautiful than the glint of the jewels.

Then the servants piled gold coins atop the jewels. "Here, take the jewels and the coins."

"No," she said, "I want the baby." And she thought how the sound of her baby's laughter was far more beautiful than the clink of the golden coins.

At last the king said, "All right then, you can have the baby. Now hand over the harp."

But she had come so far; she wasn't going to be tricked now.

"The baby first," she said, holding as tightly to the harp as she could.

"The harp first," he said.

"The baby first."

And finally, knowing that if he wanted the harp he would have to take the girl with it, the fairy king motioned to his servants, and they brought out the baby.

She took the baby with one arm and handed over the harp with the other.

The king set his fingers to the strings, and the sound was so pure and filled with joy that all the fairies gathered round to listen, forgetting all about the girl and her baby.

They walked out of the enchanted circle and all the way home to the fisherfolk who'd been so kind. And there they lived to the end of their days.

STORY:
The Spark that Kindles Imagination

⋅⫶⋅

ONE MORNING on the way to school, after working all weekend on the beginning of this book, I described the project to my eleven-year-old son Jonah. "I want to explain to teachers what storytelling teaches children," I said.

His quick-fire response was, "Well, then you will have to write a chapter about imagination."

"What does storytelling have to do with imagination?" I asked him.

"If you listen to the story of Robin Hood," he said, "You can act out the story when you play."

Jonah, who has listened to all my stories and cannot go to sleep without hearing a portion of a book every night, has always used a great deal of imagination in his play. Blocks, action figures, and costumes have been only props, while his imagination has been the impetus and focus of his play. When he was a young child, he often led other children into the worlds he created, modeling and instilling in his friends another way to spend their time.

"Do you think," I asked, "that being Robin Hood as a child may mean anything to you when you grow up?"

"I'll be able to tell the story to my own children," he

said. "I know a lot of stories."

"What about the kind of person you become," I persisted. "Do you think Robin Hood and the other stories will have any influence on who you will be?"

"Yes," he said, without skipping a beat. "It's hard to explain, but it's something like this. If you just hear a story and you imagine it, you can take something you like from a person in a story and put it into yourself."

I went straight home to write down what Jonah had said because he had so effortlessly captured the powerful link of stories to imagination. Like the resourceful mother in *The Lost Child*, he realized that we carry the riches of our imagination wherever we go in life, but where we go may well be determined by our capacity to imagine. The imagination is light baggage, as that mother in *The Lost Child* discovered, but it succeeded in carrying her to fairyland and back.

Imagination is given fairly short shrift in an educational system that demands high proficiency in reading, writing, math, and computer skills along with knowledge of science, social science, and foreign languages. Perhaps educators pay less attention to imagination because they would be hard-pressed to measure it at a time when we seem destined to emphasize those skills that we can most easily assess. In spite of this, I would like to suggest that, in addition to remembering facts and solving problems, it is essential for teachers to consider whether the students entrusted to their care are using their imaginations and entering the world with a sense of wonder. Storytelling offers a dynamic method for exercising, developing, and nurturing children's imaginations that can provide a foundation for thinking and a source of creativity and hope.

What is this elusive thing we call "imagination"? Dictionary definitions describe both the positive and negative connotations; the creative power of imagination contrasts with the "foolish notions and empty fancies." A third definition calls attention to "resourcefulness in dealing with new or unusual experiences."

Laura Sewall, a visual scientist, calls imagination "a mode of consciousness." She writes, "Empowered by imagination, we become active translators—we soak in one reality and may spin it back with a strand of beauty woven into the fabric."

The acts of storytelling and story listening require that we actively engage this "mode of consciousness" called imagination. To tell a story well, storytellers rely on their vivid imaginations to see through the characters' eyes, feel their emotions, and walk the terrain of the story's landscape. As we weave a story, it is our personal visioning and understanding—both emotional and intellectual—that creates an almost palpable reality for the listener. As tellers we must see and feel what we are expressing in order for the experience to transfer to the listeners' imaginations.

Children who listen to stories often say that they feel as if the story has come alive. One fifth grader I worked with wrote, "To me it feels like I'm right there when it happens," and another said, "It felt like I was in the story. I closed my eyes and imagined it. In my imaginings everything looked so beautiful. In my imaginings a very old town turns into a beautiful palace."

The most effective storytellers carry within them an ineffable quality that makes this magical experience possible: a sense of wonder. For a listening child, a story enters consciousness at the place where imagination intersects with a sense of wonder. The sense of wonder that pervades all good storytelling is responsible both for the story's magical qualities and for the deep and lasting impression it makes upon the listener's memory and imagination.

Rachel Carson captures the essence of a storyteller's work with children in her essay *A Sense of Wonder*:

> *If I had influence with the good fairy who is supposed to preside over the christening of all children I should ask that her gift to each child be a sense of wonder so indestructible that it would last throughout life, as an unfailing antidote against the boredom and disenchantment of late years, the sterile preoccupation with things that are artificial, the alienation from the sources of our strength.*

THE IMAGINATION required of a story listener parallels that of the teller. In fact, the ephemeral and nonmaterial art form of storytelling cannot take place without both teller and listener. The listener is the co-creator. Although we can conjure the gift of story only if there is someone to listen, we can neither know nor control what happens in the imagination of the listener. Like bells made of various shapes and materials, the story resonates differently with each listener because the tuning of our imaginations is determined by our past experiences and our emotional sensibilities. Imagination allows us to perceive, in our very own way, even what we have never known firsthand.

When we listen to stories, our imaginations must create the scenery and emotional landscape of the tale. Unlike literature which is filled with numerous concrete details that awaken sensory imagery for a reader, the details in an oral story are spare and suggestive. The teller may speak of a tall tree, and the listener fills in the shape of the leaves and branches, the height of the tree; or we may mention a large horse, and like a child with a coloring book, the listener sees a colored horse of his/her own choosing. The storyteller's variations in tone, volume, and pacing, our facial expressions and subtle changes in posture add cues to the listener's imagination, giving form to the spoken word. When a storyteller points above her head and says, "The rain clouds gathered above the deserted hut," like magic, we see those clouds and hut beneath, and for that moment, we do not see the storyteller at all.

A passage in Frances Hodgson Burnett's *The Little Princess* captures the feeling of storyteller and listener as they are simultaneously swept away by a tale as the book's protagonist, Sara Crewe, tells a story:

> *Anyone who has been at school with a teller of stories knows...how he or she is followed about and besought in a whisper to relate romances; how groups gather round and hang on the outskirts of the favored party in the hope of being allowed to join it and listen. Sara not only could tell stories, but she adored telling them. When she sat or stood in the midst of a circle and began to invent wonderful things, her green eyes grew big and shining, her cheeks flushed, and without knowing that she was doing it she began to act and made what she told lovely or alarming by the raising or dropping of her voice, the bend and sway of her slim body, and the dramatic movement of her hands. She forgot that she was talking to listening children; she saw and lived with the fairy folk, or the kings and queens and beautiful ladies, whose adventures*

she was narrating. Sometimes when she had finished her story, she was quite out of breath with excitement and would lay her hand on her thin little quick-rising chest, and half laugh as if at herself. 'When I am telling it,' she would say, 'it doesn't seem as if it was only made up. It seems more real than you are—more real than the school-room. I feel as if I were all the people in the story—one after the other...'

STORYTELLERS OFTEN feel young children surrender completely to the world of the story. Some children mirror a teller's movements without realizing it. After one telling they sometimes remember precise language and inflections, correcting the storyteller when he/she improvises in subsequent tellings. My colleague Jim Rohe told me once that in a second telling of a story a preschool child interrupted with, "No, the broom wasn't in that corner, it was over there," pointing to the invisible broom at the other side of the room.

Paradoxically, folktales are most real when we imagine them. When they are reduced to animated cartoons, it is as if the fairy magic vanishes. These stories are meant to be heard and not seen, so that they can be invented anew in every mind that hears them. When they take material form, as in a cartoon or a Disney movie, they lose their own transformative power.

The emotional investment that a listener makes in co-creating a story may account for the indelible fingerprint that stories seem to make on memory. Teachers frequently show surprise when their students remember the stories they have heard from a storyteller weeks, months, and even years after the telling.

In order for a story to take hold in the imagination, after

children listen, sometimes they need time just to sit with it and meditate upon it. In our culture we are not accustomed to allowing ourselves and others this time for silence and quiet integration of ideas. We either ask questions very quickly or move on to the next activity.

Sometimes I give my students a small piece of clay to make into something from the story as they think about it. Other times, I have paper and markers or crayons, so that they can draw something that they're thinking about. Older children can write in their journals. A quiet piece of music after a story can also enable them to stay within the imaginative space long enough to more fully integrate it without being asked questions that will abruptly pull them out of the state of reverie that story listening produces.

Asking children to exercise their imaginations through story listening and reflection, by vividly picturing the worlds of folktales, sharpens their ability to envision, preparing them not only for reading (something I will discuss more fully in the next chapter), but for thinking. In a world of visual media that surrounds children almost constantly with TV, movies, videos, DVD's, and video games, children receive images passively. However, story listening requires active envisioning, a necessary ingredient for creative thinking.

The ultimate act of envisioning and effecting change is the creative work of the visionary. When Martin Luther King said, "I have a dream," his imagination transformed American social history forever. Our ability to be creative in the world, in both large and small ways, is fueled by our capacity to imagine. The finest practitioners of every vocation—from the more familiar work of cooks, gardeners, and tailors, to the artistic work of painters, dancers, and writers, to the scientific work of inventors, mathematicians, and architects—all use imagination fueled by a sense of wonder.

SINCE BOTH storytelling and imagination are sometimes misperceived as fanciful and therefore without value, I want to briefly acknowledge the negative connotation of those who consider imagination "empty fancy." People sometimes assume that what is imaginary, or a figment of imagination, is not to be taken seriously. If we were to go along with that, we would have to dismiss all fantasy literature and fairytales and a great deal of fiction and poetry. Good literature, fairytales, poetry, and folktales, although grounded in reality, are also metaphors. Over the years as I have told stories to children and adults, I have come to believe that children seem to intuitively recognize metaphoric truth, sometimes more easily than adults.

In folktales the archetypal images of queens and kings, poor woodcutters and rich merchants, witches and fairies, tricksters and wise folk are not the stuff of daily reality, yet they contain lively metaphors for human emotions, character types, dilemmas, hopes, wishes, dreams, and fears. As poets teach us, it is often through metaphor that we experience our deepest connections to truth. Novelist John Gardner wrote, "The characters' actions—the plot of the tale—may or may not obey the laws of cause or effect operative in the actual world, but even when they do not, they seem natural because of their psychological or poetic truth. The reality of the world of the tale, in other words, is that of a moral universe. What ought to happen, possible or not, does happen."

When young children hear about the Little Red Hen who cannot get any of her friends to help her plant, water, mill the grain or make the bread, they can easily relate to the simple refrains "Not I," followed by "Then I will do it myself." These are concepts that are both compelling and familiar to their lives. The child's mind is not literal and does not ask, "Why are chickens and pigs talking?" Such make believe is natural and real. Grownups who have lost that flexibility of imagination are more likely to ask such questions.

As the children grow older and the tales they hear grow more complex, it is inevitable that some eight and nine year old children, after a hearing a fairytale, will ask if it's true. The moments of story listening are so very real, just as dreams are real to us while we are sleeping, that sometimes children are mystified by the differences between what is imaginary and what is real. When this question arises, I notice that some of the more worldly children smirk at the question while others cock their heads in anticipation, gratified that someone else has had the courage to ask.

I do not want the children to summarily dismiss the story as untrue and therefore without worth, and so I tell them what I believe: "The story contains a great deal of truth." Indeed, I would not tell the story if this were not the case. I once heard another storyteller say, "My story doesn't have to have happened to be true." And yet another says more simply, "All my stories are true."

In describing how good storytelling pulls us into the truth of an entirely different world, J.R.R. Tolkien wrote,

> Children are capable, of course, of literary belief when the story-maker's art is good enough to produce it. That state of mind has been called 'willing suspension of disbelief.' But this does not seem to me a good description of what happens. What really happens is that the story-maker

proves a successful 'subcreator.' He makes a secondary world which your mind can enter. Inside it, what he relates is 'true': it accords with the laws of that world. You therefore believe it, while you are, as it were, inside. The moment disbelief arises, the spell is broken; the magic, or rather art, has failed.

There is, indeed, much truth embedded in the metaphor of folktales. Fairytales, the most fanciful stories in folk literature, have elements of magic that distinguish them from other tales, and yet the characters capture a very real sense of longing and desire in their grand quests. Storyteller and folklorist Idries Shah wrote of this phenomenon, "Many traditional stories have a surface meaning (perhaps just a socially uplifting one) and a secondary, inner significance, which is rarely glimpsed consciously, but which nevertheless acts powerfully upon our minds."

Emily Dickinson could have been referring to the metaphoric power of such stories when she wrote:

Tell all the Truth but tell it slant-
Success in Circuit lies
Too bright for our infirm Delight
The Truth's superb surprise
As Lightning to the Children eased
With explanation kind
The Truth must dazzle gradually
Or every man be blind-

Storytelling provides a foundation for imagination in young children that can inspire their creative play, as my son Jonah mentioned when he said he could become Robin Hood in his play. I have wondered whether long-term storytelling in the classroom affords young children the same opportunity, and my colleagues in Storytelling Arts and I have attempted to find out. Although the storytellers can clearly observe how children respond *during* the storytelling sessions, we needed to know if there was any evidence that the children referred to stories *after* our visits. In our long-term preschool work we have been collecting written teacher observations for several years, asking teachers to record whether their students incorporate story elements during free playtime.

Teachers have provided many such instances including watching students, unassisted, act out stories on playground equipment and in free play areas such as dress up corner, kitchen, and sand box. For example, students have pretended the dolls from the dollhouse must climb the beanstalk, or they have built houses with blocks and pretended to blow them down like the big bad wolf. The children have been observed using puppets and magnets to retell stories, and one child even told the story to her doll just before naptime. Teachers have frequently noticed the children using the repetitive phrases, songs, and chants from the stories as they play.

One preschool teacher with whom we worked for a year had both a morning and afternoon preschool class, but only the morning class had weekly storytelling sessions. When the year was over she wrote that her afternoon children rarely played in the puppet and dress up corners, while the morning children used these areas frequently. When she did observe the afternoon class using the puppets, they usually fought over them without reenacting stories. The teacher also noticed that the afternoon class played with the puppets in a literal way while the morning students were more flexible in their play. They used their imaginations by allowing the puppets to stand in for many different characters in the stories.

If we think of the somewhat old-fashioned term "make-believe," we see that it is really a verb that has come to be used as a noun. The term captures the essence of children's dramatic play as a conscious act of pretending, by making something fanciful into something real. Stories provide abundant scripts for such make-believe.

Stories also have the potential to exercise a child's imagination far beyond the momentary conjuring of the story world. For many children who have little exposure to literature or travel, stories provide an opportunity to visit unknown worlds, to watch characters make difficult choices, to hear voices of wisdom. Through stories, we are invited to enter into the "realms of possibility," described by Laura Sewall:

> *A finely tuned imagination is informed by the physical world, drawing from the past and present, and from the edges of our awareness. At the edges of our visual field and at the edges of our consciousness, the world is almost but not quite known. The edge is where our known experience becomes flavored with the unknown, where imagination steps forward into the realm of possibility.*

CHILDHOOD IS not an easy time, even though we tend to romanticize it. All children, even those who have stable lives, must learn to survive disappointment, loss, and change. Some children experience poverty, abuse, neglect, violence, and despair. The regular "folk," the early tellers of the folktale, faced similar hardships. They struggled with survival but were sustained by the hope and faith that they could survive with grace. The downtrodden always overcome insurmountable obstacles in these stories, and the heroes are the poor, generous, unappreciated, and abandoned. In folktales, greed is ultimately one's undoing, but the one who gives is the one who receives endlessly. Children need to hear these stories, for they are instruments of hope.

When the mother in *The Lost Child* feels she has nothing left in the world, she reaches to her innermost self, and there, in her imagination, she remembers the stories she once heard. The images she rediscovers give her the inspiration to create the gifts she needs to get her child back, but the most important gift in this story is not the cloak or the harp but the power of imagination itself.

Folktales are also markedly different from the many violent images that flood children's imaginations if they are indiscriminately exposed to media. Many of these images, such as those on the nightly news, are violent, stark, or harsh, numbing us with their relentlessness. When a particularly horrific event happens in the world, I prefer to inform myself through the newspaper or the radio because I find the violent images too difficult to endure. Although folk and fairytales are not without their grim and even gruesome events, a sensitive storyteller will select material that is suitable for the age group she is telling to, and a child can imagine as much as his or her own imagination allows without the unedited brutality of what might flicker by on the TV, video, or movie screen. Ultimately, whatever happens in the folktale is life affirming.

After listening to a Chinese fairytale, a fifth grade girl in Trenton, New Jersey wrote, "What I felt was I can live in this world without being scared. I see a lot of colors. I love the way the environment was so nice. No trash on the ground. I didn't see nobody throw stuff out the car. It was beautiful."

Through imagining another world, through living another's choice, through overcoming another's obstacles, stories help children, especially those who face difficult lives, to know that there are possibilities beyond the neighborhood. Folktales carry this message: there is a world elsewhere. For such children, a story may make all the difference in the world. If, and only if, they have the capacity to imagine another life for themselves, will they be able to create that life.

Several years ago my colleague Joanne Epply-Schmidt and I shared a session of Langston Hughes stories and poetry with teenagers at the Mercer County Youth Detention Center. Several months later when the students were filling out evaluation forms about the storytelling program, one student wrote at the end of his form, "P.S. My dream will not be deferred." As we focus on the dilemmas of characters in making choices, we hope that the students will see that there are often more choices than meet the eye, and the wise choice may be the less evident one. Stories teach us to look beyond the obvious.

IMAGINATION IS the place within us that not only records our experiences but makes them uniquely our own. In imagination, we can picture what might have been different in the past and what might be different in the future. Without it, we could not dream, and without dreaming, we would have no power to envision life's possibilities.

Tunisian storyteller Nacer Khemir wrote, "Children have a welcoming imagination; sometimes from a story they make their most beautiful dreams. I sow in their memory stories like seeds which will bear their fruits later on." Teachers can plant these seeds for children. As they listen to stories, children use their imaginations to conjure the story's visual images, to empathize and understand, to consider choices that the characters have made or might make. Finally, they may store the tale in memory, perhaps calling upon it later to shape the future.

PART IV

STORYTELLING
and LITERACY

The MAGIC BROCADE

A Chinese Fairytale

O nce upon a time, when magic grew like green fields of rice, there lived a mother who had three sons. Her husband had died, and she had been left to raise her sons alone. She was able to do this, for she was a weaver. With sparkling threads of gold and silver and silk of every color, she wove brocades. She wove pictures into her fine cloth, pictures that were almost life-like and strangely perfect. One had flying birds emerging from the clouds. Another was filled with mountain ranges that seemed to go on forever until they disappeared. She was an artist, and her fabrics sold for a good price. In this way she provided for her children.

One day the weaver went to a city merchant to sell a brocade that she had just completed. On her way home, she wandered through the market place. She passed by many stalls and small shops. Some sold food, others had jewelry. There were teahouses and rice merchants, fruit stands, and fishmongers. As she walked through the small alleyways, something caught her eye.

It was a painting. Hidden in the mountains at the top

of the long scroll among the light green bamboo trees, there was a mansion with a red tile roof and porches all around. It overlooked a little silver fishpond and a field of wild flowers.

As she gazed at the painting, the weaver felt it come alive inside her. She felt she herself was standing on the mansion's porch. She stood there for a long time, and then she did something that she had never done before. She took her hard-earned money, the money she was planning to use until her next brocade was finished, and she bought the painting.

When she reached home, she unrolled the scroll for her sons to see. "Look, my sons," she said. "Isn't this the most enchanting place you've ever seen? Wouldn't it be glorious to live in such a place?"

Her first son laughed and said, "Mother, there is no such place in the real world."

Her second son said, "True. Such places only exist in dreams."

But her third son understood his mother better. He said, "Mother, perhaps if you wove a copy of this painting into one of your brocades, you would feel as if you were living in it."

"Yes," she said. "That is exactly what I must do."

The very next day she bought all the thread she need-ed, and she began to weave. Every day she wove, from the moment the sun showed its face above the lowest hill until it hid its face at dusk. Every day she wove, and when the first year was over, she had only woven the mountain scene and the small green leaves at the tops of the bamboo trees.

Her first two sons came complaining. "Mother, you never sell anything any more. We must work over time to buy your rice."

"Don't mind my brothers, mother," said her third son. "It is nothing to me to chop a bit of extra wood."

Now the weaver barely slept. Instead she wove day and night. At night she burned pinewood in the fire so that she could see the fine threads. Sometimes the smoke would get into her eyes, and her tears would fall on the loom. She wove them into the silver fishpond.

Another year passed, and still she had not finished. When her two older sons mumbled and grumbled, her third son would say, "Mother, your brocade is so beautiful, the gods must be watching over your shoulder. Keep weaving and all will be well with us."

Now, at night, when the smoke from the fire got into her eyes, drops of blood would fall on her loom. She wove these into the scarlet flowers.

After three years had passed, the brocade was finally complete. The weaver cut it from her loom and took it outside, laying it gently on the ground so that she could see its glory in the full light of the sun. It was all there. The bamboo forest, the mansion with the red tile roof and the porches all around. The silver fishpond and the field of wild flowers. If the painting itself had once seemed alive to her, the brocade was otherworldly, as if the gold and silver threads were quivering with life.

As she gazed at the brocade, a gentle breeze came. It lifted the brocade from the ground, and then a powerful gust of wind blew it to the east. The weaver ran after it, but it was out of sight before she could even grab hold of a single thread.

She fainted on the hillside where her sons found her later that day. After they revived her, she told them what had happened. She said to her eldest son, "You must go in search of my brocade. It means more to me than my life." The next day the eldest boy set out. He walked east for many days, and after four weeks he came to a mountain pass. There he saw a white haired woman who sat in front of a stone house. A great stone horse stood in front of her house with its head lifted, as if it were about to eat the red fruit from the tree above.

"Where are you going, my son?" asked the old woman.

He told her the story of his mother's brocade.

"I can tell you what happened to the brocade," she said. "The fairies of Sun Mountain were so awed by its perfect beauty, they stole it."

"How do I get it back?" he asked.

"That will be very difficult," said the old woman. "You must knock out your two front teeth and place them in the mouth of this stone horse. The horse will come to life and eat ten pieces of the red fruit on this tree. You must jump on his back, and he will carry you across a mountain of flames. Even when you feel the fire biting your skin, you must not utter one cry of pain. If you do, you will be devoured by fire. Then the horse will plunge into the icy waters. You must not shudder once or you will perish and sink to the bottom of the sea."

The eldest son stood motionless and pale, fearful of what he had heard.

"Never mind," said the old woman. "You don't have to go. Here, take a box of gold instead, and go where you like."

She gave him a small metal box and when he opened it, he found, indeed, that it was filled with gold coins. He began to walk home, but then he thought to himself, "If I go home, I will have to split the gold four ways. But if I go to the city, I can keep it all for myself." And that's just what he did.

His mother waited and waited. Finally she said to her second son, "Please. Follow the trail of your brother. Bring him home, and for the sake of heaven, bring my brocade back to me."

Her second son followed the trail to the east. When he came to the mountain pass, he too met the old woman and heard what he would have to do to regain the brocade. Like his brother, he turned pale.

"Never mind," said the old woman. "Here, take a box of gold instead."

And like his brother, he turned towards the city so that he could keep the gold all for himself.

By now the weaver had grown blind from weeping. Her third son came to her and said, "Mother, let me go in search of the brocade."

"No, my son, you are all I have left in the world."

"Mother, I promise, I will come home, whether I find the brocade or not. Give me your permission, for I should not like to leave without it."

"All right, then, my son, but promise to return before the next planting of the rice or I fear I shall not live to see you again."

"I promise," he said, and then he set out, following the same path to the east that his brothers had traveled.

The third son walked more swiftly than his brothers, and in two weeks time, he reached the mountain pass. When the old woman told him what he must do to get his mother's brocade, he did not hesitate for a moment. He knocked out his two front teeth and placed them in the mouth of the stone horse. The horse came to life and ate ten pieces of red fruit from the tree above his head.

The third son jumped on the horse's back, holding tightly to its mane. The horse galloped into the forest and up ahead the boy could see a mountain glowing orange and gold, with faint blue streaks running through it. As the horse raced up the mountain of flames, the boy held on to its mane with all his might and hugged his legs against the horse's flanks. With his eyes closed and his teeth clenched, he did not utter one cry of pain.

As the horse galloped down the other side of the mountain, the boy felt the heat of the fire disappearing behind him. Then he saw a great river up ahead. The horse plunged into the water, and suddenly all sensation of fire disappeared. But the relief only lasted a moment, for then the boy was awash in cold, cold water. He felt his clothes turn to ice and stick to his body, and his hands and feet seemed to turn to ice. Remembering the words of the old woman, he held the horse as tightly as he could and clamped his mouth shut. He did not shudder. He did not shiver. Not even once.

And then the horse emerged from the icy waters, and the boy saw before him a sunlit meadow of flowers and far beyond, a palace. The horse carried him across the meadow and stopped in front of the palace gate.

When the boy entered the palace, he found himself in a great round room. A fairy came to greet him. She knew who he was before he said a word, and she told him, "We borrowed your mother's brocade. It was so beautiful, we are weaving copies of it. Tomorrow we will be finished and you can take it home to her." She gave him a place to sit in the corner of the great hall and gave him some food to eat.

In the center of the room, his mother's brocade was laid out on a platform of jade. All around it, there were fairies, perhaps as many as a hundred of them, all weaving copies of it.

The boy sat and watched them weave. When night came, they hung a huge pearl from the ceiling which lit the room so that they could continue their work. Then the boy fell asleep.

One by one the fairies finished. At last there was only one fairy left. She looked at the weaver's beautiful brocade and at her own poor copy. She knew that she would never see the original again. Taking a needle and thread of red silk, she embroidered a picture of herself into the original brocade. Then she too vanished.

In the morning when the boy awoke, he found the hall empty except for his mother's brocade. He folded it gently and tucked it beneath his shirt. When he went outside, he found the horse waiting for him at the gate.

He jumped on its back, and once again it plunged into the icy sea and galloped back through the mountain of flames. When they reached the mountain pass, the old woman was waiting. "Ah, you are back already," she said, and with one quick movement, she took the teeth from the horse's mouth and put them back in the boy's mouth. Once again the horse turned to stone.

"Wait here," she said. She went inside her small cottage and brought out a pair of shoes made of light, soft leather. "Put these shoes on," she said, "and you shall reach your own home very swiftly."

In no time at all the boy was back at his mother's gate. He went into the house and found his mother lying on her bed.

"Mother," he said, "mother, wake up. I'm back. I have it. I have your brocade."

She opened her eyes, and when she saw the glistening threads, her sight came back to her.

"Let us take the brocade outside," she said, "so that we may see it in the light."

Together they spread the brocade on the ground, and it was just as she remembered.

As they looked at it, a gentle breeze came and lifted the

brocade from the ground. Another wind came and spread the brocade very wide and spread it very long; it spread the brocade until it covered the whole countryside. Then all the threads quivered, and it burst into life.

It was all there. The bamboo forest. The mansion with the red tile roof and the porches all around. The little silver fishpond and the meadow of wild flowers. But there was something there that had not been in the original, for the fairy who had embroidered herself into the brocade was now standing, dressed in red, beside the fishpond.

"Mother," said the third son. "Remember the painting you found in the marketplace so long ago? Let us hang it in the entry of our new home so that we will always remember how we came to be here."

They did so, and the weaver, her son, and the fairy who became his wife lived in that enchanted and strangely perfect place for all the rest of their days.

MANY YEARS later two beggars passed by. At first, when they saw the grand mansion, they thought, "Surely the wealthy man who lives here will give us something." But then an odd feeling came over them. This place looked strangely familiar. Then they remembered. This was their mother's brocade, come to life.

The first two sons bowed their heads and walked away.

The VOICE
of STORY:
A Bridge to Reading

⋱

O NE NEED not be insane to hear imaginary voices. Readers and writers do it every day. Indeed, in order to learn to be a reader or a writer, we must imagine the voice of language in our minds, whether it be the voice of the text we read or the voice of the text we write.

Eudora Welty explains this phenomena of voice in her autobiography *One Writer's Beginnings*:

> *Since being read to and after, when I began reading to myself, there has never been a line read that I didn't hear. As my eyes followed the sentence, a voice was saying it silently to me. It isn't my mother's voice, or the voice of any person I can identify, certainly not my own. It is human, but inward, and it is inwardly that I listen to it. It is to me the voice of the story or the poem itself. The cadence, whatever it is that asks you to believe, the feeling that resides in the printed word, reaches me through the reader-voice. I have supposed, but never found out, that this is the case with all readers—to read as listeners—and with all writers, to write as listeners. It may be part of the desire to write. The sound of what falls on the page begins the process of testing it for truth, for me.*

I have worked as a guest storyteller in many classes where children struggle with reading, and I have come to believe that storytelling can be a mediating language between the spoken and written word. The voice of the oral storyteller is neither identical to the voice of ordinary conversation nor to the voice of the written word. Rather, in its artfulness, it borrows a bit of both. Storytellers combine some conventions of literature including dialogue, traditional narrative structure, and repetitive phrasing with some of the conventions of conversation including eye contact, informal diction, and the flexibility to alter the language to suit the situation at hand. For children, both the very young who have not yet learned to read and the older children who may be struggling to make sense of words on a page, the voice of the storyteller helps them to hear the inner voice that Eudora Welty writes about, "the voice of the story or the poem itself," the voice that readers hear.

Children who are not exposed to books at home sometimes find it difficult to hear the reader's voice that Eudora Welty refers to, the "human but inward" voice that readers hear. Some educators believe that the best way to acculturate such children is through exposing them to a print-rich environment, and the benefits of reading aloud to children are absolutely essential to their development as readers. But storytelling offers a different experience that can be the missing piece for children who have difficulty connecting to the written word. By internalizing the voice of story along with the social and emotional relationships embedded in the storytelling experience, children can later transfer this experience to the culture of reading. Through listening to the oral tale, children learn to connect to literature, to discover its significance to their own lives, and to perceive the joy and meaning that is carried through language, both spoken and written.

Reading and writing are extremely sophisticated forms of communication because so much is left to the imagination. Writers assume the presence of their audience, but they cannot see them and do not know them. Readers, likewise, must imagine the writer speaking to them. The writer cannot hear the reader thinking, and the reader cannot respond directly to the writer. For children, it is a cognitive leap to enter and engage in the sophisticated but invisible dialogue of written text. By contrast, storytelling makes both sides of this dialogue real to children who are engaging in actual communication with the storyteller and the text of the story.

This act of communication resembles the creativity described in *The Magic Brocade* when the widow's brocade comes to life. The storyteller, like the widow who recreates a beautiful painting in her weaving, brings a story to life through the deep work of imagination. The listeners, like the third son and the fairies who enter and reside in the scene of the brocade, experience the life-like quality of the story's imaginary world.

By embodying language in a physical, emotional, and oral form, public storytelling mimics written literature, adding to it a palpable sense of intimacy. Writers also strive for this sense of intimacy, but children cannot see and feel it without a lot of practice. For sophisticated readers, text comes to life in their mind's eye, just as a story comes to life for the listener. Storytelling models this imaginative process.

Storytelling also serves as an alternate route to teaching literacy that can reach children who have been failed by the more conventional methods. It can break through cultural barriers that can sometimes prevent children from connecting to the written word and support the comprehension skills that make text meaningful. Indeed, stories can circumvent the pervasive problems of disconnection, passivity, and alienation, like water flowing around rocks.

There is a massive cultural barrier, invisible to some teachers, that stands in the way of literacy for some children, particularly those who do not come from mainstream American culture. Victoria Purcell-Gates writes about such learners in her book *Other People's Words*, a study of an illiterate urban Appalachian family whose cultural discourse does not include written materials of any kind. She argues that rather than thinking of such people as "language deprived," as has sometimes been suggested, we must consider that reading and writing are simply not part of some cultures, even in contemporary America.

Granted, reading and writing are so widely practiced in America and so necessary to master in order to succeed in mainstream culture, we sometimes forget that literacy may not be the norm for everyone. In fact, for some people, written materials are both inaccessible and profoundly alienating. The first grade child Purcell-Gates works with does not understand at first that writing is a symbolic system, and once he learns this, he continues to avoid reading because of the strong identification he has with his father who does not read. His mother so deeply doubts her own ability to read that she struggles to find the confidence to decode language, even after nine years of schooling.

Children who come from cultures where the oral tradition is more important than the written are deeply engaged by storytelling. That is why, when I visit classrooms in urban

New Jersey schools, I always have the feeling that the language of story is a language that the children know, understand, and feel comfortable with. These children need to hear live stories from their teachers in order to learn. The personal voice of story can bring a new dimension to what would otherwise appear to them as cold and lifeless print, lifeless because they have not yet learned to hear the voice inside the text, the voice that the storyteller can teach them to hear. Most children enjoy hearing stories, but for children who do not easily connect to the written word, stories can be the bridge to literacy.

A few years ago a Princeton University student came to observe my work in the Trenton schools. She was a Native American from a Pueblo tribe in New Mexico, and she needed no explanation of the value of oral storytelling; it was part of her personal heritage. When I asked her if the stories of her people were written down, she said, "Oh, no. We would never write down our stories. We believe that a story is alive as the breath is alive. If we write it down, it dies."

In *Mosaic of Thought*, an insightful and practical book on teaching reading comprehension, Ellin Oliver Keene and Susan Zimmerman speak about the lack of engagement and passivity that some children show around books. "My concern is that many children are not so engaged as they read. They don't know when they're comprehending. They don't know when they're not. They don't know whether it's critical for them to comprehend a given piece. And if they don't comprehend, they don't know what to do about it. . . . Many don't seem to know that they can expect text and pictures to have meaning, and that the meaning is inherently interesting and worth paying attention to." Likewise, teachers sometimes tell me that when they read aloud to children, they cannot keep the children's attention.

Quite the opposite is true when children listen to stories told to them. They listen with enthusiasm, excitement, and energy. The children who sit on the floor tilt forward on their knees, soaking up every word. The authentic emotional engagement that the storyteller shows for the story transfers easily to the child. In fact, I often notice that some children listen in spite of their desire not to. This is particularly true at the Mercer County Detention Center where some of the new boys may be initially resistant to the stories but within moments forget themselves in their desire to listen. Surprisingly, even the ones who do their best to "show" they're not listening will later correct their classmates for "retelling it wrong."

In addition to helping children cross the cultural divide, storytelling can also help children who carry negative attitudes towards reading. Sometimes teachers tell me that certain children are extremely challenging: they cannot read, cannot sit still, cannot listen, cannot attend, cannot learn. Surprisingly, these are usually the same children who sit most attentively for stories, whose eyes sparkle when they listen, who offer insights during discussion that make the teacher's jaw drop. I know that storytelling is a language that excites and inspires them when these children stop me in the hall and ask, "Are you coming to see me today?" I know that the story has made a difference when the children remember the details of stories, even years later. I know that stories are a language that disarms and captivates when virtually all behavior problems vanish as they listen.

These children want to listen to stories. They want to

retell. And finally, they want to get their hands on books that have stories like the ones I tell them. The pages of a book are not magical if the children do not first "hear" the magic from someone who believes in it. The storyteller's authentic and powerful engagement with the material serves as a model for how to engage with literature through hearing the voice, feeling the emotion, and carrying the meaning. The ability of the tale to engage a child both emotionally and intellectually, gives us the opportunity to involve students in a cycle of learning about language that is highly replicable when we turn to the printed word.

When I was working with a Trenton elementary school third grade class, I told the story of *Rumplestiltskin,* which none of the children had heard before. The following week when I returned, a little boy named Elijah came up to me and said, "Can I tell the story today?"

"Which story would you like to tell?" I asked him.

"The one you told last week," he said.

He proceeded to stand before the class and tell an animated and completely coherent version of *Rumplestiltskin* that amazed me with its detail and rhythm. After class I asked for permission to take Elijah on a visit to the school library's folklore section. "These stories," I told him, "are like the story you told today." His eyes grew big as a child's in a candy store. He had no idea that such treasures could be found in books. When the storyteller shares a story, it is a treasure. The children know this without being told and can be prepared to mine the treasure for themselves.

In *Mosaic of Thought* Ellin Oliver Keene and Susan Zimmerman begin with the premise that many children can decode language successfully but do not understand what they are reading. By studying the thought processes that proficient readers use, they create a model of how children can be taught to think as they read. The teacher models a thinking strategy as she reads aloud to children, and gradually the children learn to apply the strategy to their own reading. Teachers demonstrate how to differentiate between what we understand and don't understand; how we think about what we read in relationship to what we already know; how we create images in our minds as we read; how we ask questions as we read; and how we synthesize ideas to create meaning. All of these thinking skills can be taught through story listening, and some are integral to the experience because of the children's active engagement. In fact, teachers can quite easily guide children to practice these comprehension skills as they engage in story listening.

I often tell repetitive tales to young children such as *The Three Bears*, *The Three Billy Goats Gruff*, and *The Little Red Hen*, stories with predictable refrains. While I tell these stories, I ask the children to join in when they know what to say, even if they haven't heard the story before. Three and four year old children are able to do this, showing their ability to predict, an important skill in reading comprehension.

They also begin to guess what's going to happen, even when it is not part of a repetitive pattern. Some years ago I was telling Sam McBratney's *Guess How Much I Love You* to a Head Start class. The story is about a big hare and a little hare who are comparing how much they love each other. The little hare opens his arms wide and shows the big hare how much he loves him, but the big hare, in turn, opens his arms even wider. Each time the little hare thinks of something he can do to show his great affection, the big hare is able to do it even bigger, showing that he loves the little bunny even more. Towards the end of the story the big hare says, "I love you across the river and over the hills."

As I was telling the story, just at this point, a little boy named Jamir was getting more and more involved and blurted out, "I love my daddy all the way to heaven." Indeed, he had guessed where the story was going, for the next line in the story is, "I love you right up to the moon." For Jamir, the story was so immediate and real, he knew that big hare was his daddy. He also displayed his understanding of the theme of the story by finding the vastest metaphor for love that he could imagine.

In addition to predicting what was going to happen in the story, Jamir was doing something else that is essential to good readers. He was automatically relating the text of the story to himself. Good readers are in constant dialogue with text. They know that what they read has meaning for them, and they find the meaning through relating what they know already to what they read. Jamir knew that this story was about the love between him and his father, and he so completely identified with the little hare in the story that he could not contain his enthusiasm about his love for his daddy.

A third comprehension component that Jamir was experiencing was his visualization of the story. Good readers must imagine what they're reading, and children can learn to do this through listening. As I discussed in the preceding chapter, imagination is key to story listening. Once our imaginations are engaged, we make the story we hear our own. The images may be inspired by the words of the story and the tone of voice and gestures of the teller, but they are created inside the mind of the listener. Likewise, good readers must learn to imagine what they read, but they cannot do this until they can imagine that the voice of the text is as alive and immediate as the one they hear from the storyteller.

As I told *The Three Bears* to another Head Start class, the children, who had never heard it before, were entranced. When I got to the part where the bears come home and Papa Bear says, "Who's been eating my porridge," a little boy named Dante said, "How did he know?"

Well, I'd never thought about that before, even after a lifetime of knowing the story, and said, "You know, that's a great question. How do you think he knew?"

"There was a little less in the bowl," he said.

"And maybe the spoon was dirty," said another.

When I got to the part where Mama Bear says, "Someone's been sitting in my chair," Dante piped up again, "How did she know?"

No one was sure about this so I suggested, "Maybe there was a soft pillow in the middle of her chair, and there was a dent in it."

And finally when the bears went upstairs and Papa Bear says, "Someone's been sleeping in my bed," Dante asked again, "How did he know?"

"The covers were all messed up," someone suggested.

"I know," said someone else. "The pillow was on the floor. My pillow sometimes falls on the floor when I'm sleeping."

Readers often think of questions as they read. Sometimes we ask literal questions that can be answered by the text if we read carefully, and sometimes the questions go beyond the text. Some of the questions are ultimately unanswerable, but still worth asking. Four-year-old Dante was so intent in his listening, that his questions about the bears were totally authentic and compelling. He had to know. Storytelling gives us the opportunity to teach children to ask meaningful questions, before, during, and after the story.

These can be questions about the world of the story and its culture; but they can also be the big questions about life itself, since every tale raises its share of them. For example, *The Magic Brocade* might raise questions such as these: *How do people in the same family grow into such different people? Is goodness always rewarded? Does love need to be tested? If you sow greed, what do you get in return?* Brainstorming the life questions in a single fairytale, I have had a group of fifteen teachers come up with more than fifty questions.

Stories can provide us a way for asking questions, beginning at a very young age. By teaching them the skill of questioning, we validate a child's curiosity even if we do not know the answer. Cultivating an inquiring mind is a thinking skill that will help children with both textual skills and daily life.

As they listen and become deeply engaged in stories, children can retell those stories, create variants, and find the stories in their own lives that remind them of the stories they hear. By making the storyteller's voice their own, they are able to develop clear articulation and logical sequencing. They begin to realize that the nuance of tone affects meaning, in stories and in conversation. Mostly, they realize that they have a voice and something worth saying, for by telling stories to them, we are inviting them to do the same.

THE TRADITIONAL Armenian folktales ends, "Three apples fell from heaven: one for the storyteller, one for the listener, and one for the one who heard." When children listen to stories, they really hear, and in hearing they can begin to think, to understand, and to find meaning in language. For some, this will open the door to literacy.

The VOICE
of STORY:
A Bridge to Writing

⋅⋮⋅

RECENTLY I was visiting a fifth grade class for two weeks to teach writing through storytelling. It was springtime, and a boy in one of the front seats sauntered in late and seemed to flaunt his disinterest in school. But when I began to tell a story, I knew I had him. When I asked the students to discuss the story, he had his hand up for every question. And when I asked them to write, he did. His teacher told me that it was the first time that the child had invested himself in anything all year.

Through my own work and the work of my colleagues, I have come to believe that storytelling is a powerful way to teach writing. I have seen it motivate children, increase their fluency, lend form to their writing, and give them the confidence that they have something to say. Although I know it works, I have also puzzled over why it works. In this chapter I would like to suggest that by using storytelling as a prewriting activity, the storyteller's voice and the emotional experience of the story motivate and inspire young writers to pick up their pencils and record thoughts, images, feelings, and memories. My discussion will not address the mechanics of writing, revision or editing—equally important phases that occur later in the writing process. Instead I will focus on the elements of fluency and form.

Like reading, writing is a silent language that children must practice first through hearing and speaking. They must learn to consciously hear their own voices before they can write, just as they must hear the voice of prose in their minds in order to make sense of the symbolic language of reading. The storytelling voice, which resembles the voice of written narrative, helps them move from spoken to written language because it embodies the elements of narrative: its shape, feeling, pacing, dialogue. Young writers must be able to hear the language of literature spoken in a natural way and speak that language aloud before they can be expected to hear the language in their minds. Hearing the storyteller's voice and imitating it, students can begin to discover their writing voices.

Once again, we can compare this process to the metaphor in *The Magic Brocade.* The fairies love the artistry of the brocade, and they try to copy it, reminding us that we learn the tools of our craft, whatever it may be, through imitation. The fairies' imitations are not as grand as the widow's because they do not have her experience. In this way the fairies resemble our students. They model what we offer them, but at first, their efforts may be poor copies. Their work gains meaning over time as they place themselves into the stories, like the fairy who joins the old woman and her son at the end. Our stories become their stories. Listening and responding, their voices come to life.

When we tell stories to children, we give them opportunities to internalize the stories, weaving the strands of the tales with their own life experiences. This process of engaging in dialogue with the story through the storyteller helps children learn how to make meaning. When they begin to use their own expressive language to talk and write, voicing their memories and ideas, whatever has taken life in their imaginations is transformed into creative expression.

How does this work? If we consider the elements that create oral narrative and written narrative, we see that some of the tools of storytelling and writing are different. In order to communicate a story effectively, storytellers use facial expression, gestural and postural movement, eye contact, and four aspects of voice—tone, volume, pacing, and pitch. Without access to vocal and kinesthetic expression, writers must learn to finely hone their choice of words. Storytellers can see their audience and communicate directly, improvising to adjust to audience reaction. Writers, by contrast, must imagine their readers and understand what those invisible readers already know or don't know. Storytellers voice their words, while writers must learn to hear the sound of their own voices in their minds as they write, capturing language and rhythm so precisely that readers can imagine them, too.

What the storyteller and the writer share in common are the words themselves and the desire to communicate them, and they fashion these words similarly when it comes to narrative. The difference is in the packaging. In a written story, the text is all words, but in an oral text, at least fifty percent of a storytelling performance is nonverbal. As the storyteller embodies the text, delivering the words with meaningful gesture, posture, pacing, vocal and facial expression, she not only voices the story, but shapes and interprets it, making it emotionally accessible to the children who listen. Listening to a story, young writers hear a lively narrative voice and begin to internalize its rhythms, structure, and images.

Writing teachers have known for a long time that

prewriting activities are key to releasing the writer's voice. Faced with a blank sheet of paper, most of us don't know what to say. We need a reason to write, motivation to do so, and an audience that will listen. Brainstorming, journal writing, writers' notebooks, visualization, reading, and discussion can all loosen up the threads that tie up the writer's voice. In order to write, we need to feel that we have something to say, and we need to connect emotionally to whatever that might be.

After children hear a story, their high level of engagement motivates them to write. Indeed, many teachers have told us that their students, even the reluctant writers, are more willing and eager to write after they hear a story told to them. A second grade teacher I worked with in Trenton said that after her students listened to a story, they would write more freely, rarely asking her what to say. "If I just told them to write without telling a story first," she said, "they would just write, 'I love my mommy,' and then get stuck. But if I told a story, it was as if I turned on a spigot."

There are several reasons for this level of engagement. The first goes back to my early discussion of the way that storytelling creates trusting relations between a teacher and student. Let me give you two examples. My colleague Joanne Epply-Schmidt, who tells stories weekly at a youth detention center, has told me on more than one occasion that her students have been inspired to write a memoir or poem for her to read. These boys have written about their own lives, particularly the abuse and neglect they have experienced, and some have even taken the risk—a significant risk in this setting—of sharing their writing with the class.

My colleague Paula Davidoff has used storytelling to

teach writing to teenagers who attend an alternative high school for juvenile offenders. When her program was monitored by the Juvenile Justice Commission, Paula shared the students' writing journals. The officials were astounded by the students' work because they had never before seen these young people produce any writing.

Joanne's and Paula's storytelling and their understanding of complex characters contained a subliminal message that caused the students to think, "If she can understand *those* people, maybe she can understand me, too." And not just understand, but do so without judgment, because in effective storytelling, we become the characters—we do not judge them. By trusting the discourse of storytelling, students, even those who have great resistance, can be motivated to write.

Storytelling also engages children in an active dialogue with the teller. By speaking directly to the listener—not through written words or a visual screen—the storyteller creates intimacy and the desire for direct and immediate response. Once the story has ended, dialogue with the storyteller can come in the form of talking or writing about the story.

Storytelling inspires students to write because it is truly experiential education. Although the students are not climbing mountains or diving into lakes and rivers, they are traveling in their imaginations as the storyteller triggers their sensory awareness of sight, sound, and movement. When they're in class, personal experiences can seem so distant and inaccessible that children perceive their lives as totally uneventful; there's not a thing to say. Stories, by contrast, help to bring immediate experience into the room, and after a story, students are usually bursting to write.

The last and perhaps most important reason that story-telling motivates student writing is because storytelling comes from an emotional place in the storyteller and taps channels of feeling in the listeners. When we tell stories, we imbue them with authentic feeling. Journeying with the characters, the listeners inhabit the space behind the characters' eyes, see-ing what the characters see and experiencing their emotions. Afterwards the listeners are able to recall these moments of feeling. They are also prepared to remember when they might have felt the same way. If and when writers connect to authentic feeling, they are able to release the voices within them.

Often I begin my writing workshops by asking the stu-dents to write about moments that were most vivid to them in the story they just heard. Through guided visualizations I try to trigger sensory details by asking them what they saw, heard, smelled, and touched. I ask them to notice the weath-er, the light, how people in the scene were dressed. They visu-alize one scene in their minds like the frame of a movie:

Here are three examples of student responses to *The Magic Brocade*. A fourth grader wrote,

> *I saw the third son putting his two front teeth in the horse's mouth while the old woman was looking at him. Next to the house was a tree. On the tree were silver apples. The grass was dark green. The sounds I heard were birds singing. If I was the third son I would have knocked out my two front teeth for mother because I love her.*

A fifth grade student wrote,

I pictured a big black mountain with fire all around it with a little hallway about three feet wide and a man with a long black coat on a big black horse with wings but cannot fly. It had bunny teeth. When it got to the top of the mountain it jumped head first into the icy water.

This seventh grader's response is more complex:

The mother is sitting in the darkness of a small room with a single candle glowing dimly. The only sounds are of her sons' light breathing in their sleep, and very faintly a sound like a small drop. Tears of blood and water are falling onto the brocade, and as she weaves, a certain glimmer comes over the threads, making them glow brightly, even in the dim candlelight. The red flowers in the brocade seem to sway faintly back and forth with the flickering of the candle, and a shade is on the bamboo forest.

THESE WRITERS have taken ownership of the story's images by choosing moments that are compelling to them. When they listen to one another's descriptions, they also see that the content of their imaginations and their expressive language are different. Even though they are writing about the same story, their vision is personal. Responding to the stories in this way gives students permission to voice their unique ways of perceiving the world.

Repeating an exercise like this with different stories helps increase fluency in writing, just as journal writing does. Peter Elbow teaches that fluency precedes form and correctness. Just as we learn to speak, draw, or play the piano through practice, children need time to practice writing without worrying about a final draft, a finished product, or a masterpiece. Once in a while they can revise and polish a piece, but simply practicing is equally important, especially in the development of fluency.

The Magic Brocade, like most folktales, draws bold outlines, allowing the listeners to fill in the details. You can see from these writing samples that all three students added details that were not mentioned in the story. Writing is effective when it is concrete and vivid, using specific nouns, active verbs, and dialogue, but often students write in vague language that makes their writing lifeless and disengaged. Writing about a story they've listened to gives them the opportunity to create word pictures of what they see, grasping the detail that enlivens prose. By prompting the students in the visualization exercise to notice the sensory details of the natural or manmade environments such as color, temperature, and sound, we not only increase their fluency but also begin to help them capture concrete detail necessary for strong writing.

Children have great awareness and many life experiences, but getting to their memories is a bit like playing "hide go seek." As teachers we need strategies that will help them gain access to those memories. I sometimes ask the children to reenter, what is for them, a compelling moment of the story that I've told. I guide them through another visualization, focusing at the end on the feeling of the moment. Then I ask them to recall a time in their own lives when they experienced the same feeling. Again, the immediacy of the story experience brings their feelings to the surface, giving them readier access to memory. In the many classes I have taught, I find that it is rare that a child cannot discover a little diamond of experience—a special tree, the moment spent with a grandparent, a surprising gift. The story provides an invitation to explore deeper places within the self.

Here is a poem a seventh grader wrote that was inspired by the feeling of sadness in the story she heard:

I see my mother
sitting on my bed
wearing her pink housecoat
telling me my great grandmother died
in Mississippi
and I couldn't go to the burial to pay my respects.

I remembered my great grandmother
praying with my mother
telling her how happy she was.
She was not really praying
she was singing
with a tremble in her voice
holding my mother's hand
just singing.

One of her classmates captured the feelings of fear and loneliness when he wrote:

I was little, about six.
I had locked myself in a closet.
In there it was cold
And when I called for help
The sound echoed.
The room's walls were brick.
I was sitting in there
As if I was in jail.

THE POWER of this writing stems from its simplicity, the stark clear details, and voices that ring with authentic feeling. Through working with visualization exercises related to stories they had heard, these writers were able to remember specific times and places when they had felt the same emotion as a character in the story. I simply asked them to record the picture of the feeling.

I also ask the students to avoid using the names of the feelings in their writing. If the picture is strong, it will create these feelings without "telling" the readers what they're supposed to feel. Writing becomes sentimental when we load it down with feeling words instead of strong experiences that create those feelings. Students can begin to see this in the stories they hear.

When I ask them, "How did the widow feel when her brocade was stolen?" they tell me, "Sad, heart-broken, lonely, desperate."

"How do you know that," I ask, "when I didn't tell you?" Then they begin to realize that action, dialogue, and image incorporate feeling.

A fifth grade student who related the story *Jumping Mouse* to her own life, reflected at the end of her piece how much she enjoyed sharing feeling with a story:

> *I am telling this story because it's the same as the scene in the story when the frog tells little mouse to crawl and jump as high as he can. He got scared. But then he was happy because nothing bad happened to him. That is my experience in life that was the same as Jumping Mouse. In his story some of his feelings were the same as mine. It was really fun sharing some feeling with a fiction story.*

ONCE AGAIN this student reminds us that engagement and a sense of fun are key elements in motivating student writing. Storytelling can also prepare children to write particular types of stories by modeling them first. As a beginning to story writing, I enjoy teaching students creation stories and "pour quoi stories" ("why" stories that explain things such as why grass is green, why rabbits have long ears and short tails, why tigers have stripes, etc.)

I begin by telling them several creation stories to get them thinking like mythmakers. Sometimes I ask them to close their eyes and imagine the very beginning of time and space. Children are natural wonderers. They have not forgotten to ask questions about how the world around them has come to be the way it is. Imagining the beginning of things is easy for the supple imaginations of children, especially if they are awakened by similar stories.

This seventh grade student began with a wonderful rhythm, modeled on a creation story she had listened to:

> *A long, long time ago before the animals, before the trees, before the people, before the world had come to be, a long living mystery was formed. It was ever so quiet, nothing to see but the black of the sky and sparkles of white. The air was crisp, but no one to breathe it. The surroundings were dark, but no one to see it. The world was none.*

This exercise inspired a creation poem in another seventh grade writer:

> *Thousands of years ago, before creation,*
> *There were two forms-*
> *Light and Darkness.*
> *There were two stars-*

Life and Death.
There were two gods-
Good and Evil.
Both Good and Evil, on their stars,
Rotated around one terrific force,
A black hole.
While rotating
Something unusual occurred.
The black hole became strong.
So strong that it took in both forces.
This mighty reaction
Caused a great explosion.
From this explosion,
Large bit of debris scattered.
Scattered all around the universe
Each bit, which later formed a star or planet,
Had both –
Light and Darkness,
Life and Death,
Good and Evil.
That is how our universe came to be.

A fifth grader created this piece:

*In the beginning there was nothing but water and a man.
It stayed light outside so it was easy to see. One day the
man came up to the middle of the ocean and prayed for
magic powers. He received his powers and snapped his
finger. Do you know what came up? Soil, gold, silver,
clouds, grass, and everything we have today. He snapped
a second time and up came the moon and stars and the
sun. A whole atmosphere was made. Today we call it
Earth.*

IN ALL THREE samples the writers have captured not only the tale type, but also the language and rhythm of the creation story. Listening to the tales first was key to producing these stories.

After telling creation stories, we can generate more "wondering" questions about the world, questions that people have asked since the beginning of time. Although science can now answer some of these questions, children are more like our ancient ancestors who don't yet know those answers. Some of the questions are the immense unanswerable ones. A fourth grade class generated these questions:

> *How did fish get in the water?*
> *Why is God up there and not down here?*
> *Why is the wind cold?*
> *Why is the sun shiny?*
> *Why can't people fly like a bird or hold their breath*
> *under water like fish?*
> *Why are we different colors?*
> *Why do people die of old age?*
> *Where do people go when they die?*
> *Why doesn't it hurt to have your hair cut?*
> *What makes the ocean stop at the shore?*
> *Why are tongues wet?*
> *Why is the sun so far away and it looks so close?*
> *Why is the moon different shapes sometimes?*
> *Why do people speak different languages?*

These questions can become the starting points for new stories that we can compose as a whole class, in small groups, or individually. In an exercise I called "Questions you never asked your mother, answers she never gave you," a class of seventh graders wrote this collaborative poem:

Why are there stars, moons, plants, and suns?
A god shaped all the planets, moons, stars, and suns out
of clay
Then sprinkled them with a magic powder.

Why is the earth round?
God was playing basketball and he lost the ball.
It stayed in outer space.

If you were skinny enough could you go in a telephone
and hear people talking?
Yes, but you'd have to be skinner than a snake and
smaller than a mouse.

Why is the wind invisible?
To wrap itself around us
To wrap itself around trees and clouds
To lay over rivers and oceans
and caress them all with gentle fingers
The wind enfolds the earth
It does not stifle it.

Where did we get the words we speak?
One day a man found a cave and in it were all the
words.

Why does the wind whistle when it blows through the
trees?
The wind is an angel whistling coyly while she works.

Why do clouds move?
Because when the heavens sneeze they move the clouds
along the sky with great force.

ASKING QUESTIONS such as these encourage children's natural capacity to wonder. Even young children can do this. They may not be able to write their stories down themselves, but they can create them, and you can write it down for them, read it to them, and let their text become material that they can learn to read for themselves.

In additional to mythic questions about the world, a story they've heard can also inspire children to write "stories within stories," if we teach them to ask questions that are not answered within the story. After listening to *The Magic Brocade*, for example, students asked, "Why did the boy's teeth transform the horse? What happened to the widow's husband? Why doesn't the mountain of flames burn out? Who created the mountain of flames and the icy sea and why? Why was the third son different from his brothers? What did the first two sons do when they got to the city? What did the fairies do with their copies of the brocade?"

One student posed and answered the question, "How did the fairies get on top of the mountain?"

The fairies came from heaven. They were kicked out by God as a temporary punishment for disagreeing with him. God had told the fairies to fluff up their wings and polish their halos. When they refused, God sent them out for one year. To get back to heaven they would have to help a human being on earth.

So after God sent them down, they wandered for one week until they came to a magical house. It was a very beautiful house. It was white with a fence around it and right in front there was a yard with a big pearl ball. It was not like an ordinary ball, it was a ball that lights up a night. The garden was used for the fairies so they could do their weaving.

Storytelling not only influences the content of students' writing but also its form. First and second grade teachers in Storytelling Arts programs are noticing that their students are using more narrative conventions such as beginnings, endings, detail, and dialogue. One first grade teacher commented that her students' writing "by far surpasses my classes in the past. Their sense of what makes a story, including making a beginning, middle, and end is much better. They are also using their imaginations more overall."

IN ALL OF the activities I have described, I am asking the students to engage in a dialogue with the story, and sometimes I invite them to write to me. At the end of my two weeks in a Trenton fifth grade class in 2004, I asked the students to write me a letter and tell me which was their favorite story and why. One child wrote, "Dear Susan, I liked *The Magic Brocade* the best because I liked the magic in the story and the brocade. I liked it because I just imagined seeing the way the brocade looked and how it was when it came to life. I also imagined the way he looked when he went through the burning fire and the freezing ice. I loved the way the third son believed in himself and his mom. Your Friend, M."

I was particularly touched by this letter because the teacher had told me that this child was usually not motivated or successful in his writing. Yet he not only picked up a major theme of the story but was able to use the story to see his own potential.

By visualizing the stories and capturing their images in

words, our students learn to articulate their elusive imaginings. Incorporating the structure of narrative they hear, their writing gains form. Hearing the melody of narrative in the storyteller's words, they begin to hum their own tunes because they internalize the sound, the rhythm, and meaning of language. Telling our students stories before we ask them to write, we till the soil of their imaginations and plant the seeds for their creativity.

PART V

The GIFT

The VISION in the WOOD

There was once a woodcarver who loved his craft so very much that the wood seemed to become as he wished almost by his touch. He could see the figure of a squirrel in a curved branch of a tree or a deer in the body of a fallen oak. The figures he saw in the wood seemed alive to him and when he had finished carving them, they seemed alive to those who saw them. The wood gleamed like satin; anyone who passed by had to lay a hand on these wooden creatures which felt warm and smooth as a baby's skin.

From an early age the woodcarver had known his vocation, as if there were no other choice. And he practiced it diligently for thirty years—from the time he was allowed to hold the carving tools.

But one morning he awoke, and as he looked around his studio he didn't see figures and animals waiting in the wood; he saw only wood. He tilted his head this way and that, and suddenly he realized that this was how most people saw wood. No matter how he looked at it, he couldn't see anything but wood cut from trees, motionless, lifeless.

At first he was perplexed and then angry. He picked up one of his carving knives, grabbed a slab of wood, and carved, not with his usual grace and agility but boldly and without care. As he did so the knife slipped, severely wounding his right hand, the hand that held the knife.

Perhaps it was no accident. Perhaps the hand had allowed the knife to slip on purpose. Whatever the case, his hand could not be used again—for carving or anything else.

THE WOODCARVER was able to survive by using his savings and by selling the carvings left from before the accident. Yet each morning he awoke wondering what to do. "I always knew I was made for carving wood," he told himself. "I am of no use to the world now." The passion that had motivated him all his life had disappeared as mysteriously as it had come, and no other arrived to take its place.

He lived this way for a while, wishing the days to pass quickly and the nights slowly, when one day a young man came to his door. "I wish to become a woodcarver," he said, "and I've been told you're the best this part of the world has ever seen. Will you teach me?"

"Didn't you hear about me? I can no longer carve. I've lost the use of my hand." He didn't want to say he'd lost the vision of a woodcarver, too; he'd not admitted that to anyone.

"Yes," said the young man. "I've heard about your accident. But I thought, sir, that perhaps you could teach me with words, and I will try to do as you say."

In all his working life the woodcarver had never taken an apprentice. Though he'd been asked to, he had always said he was too busy. Actually, he had no desire to have students creating works that looked like his just for the purpose of selling more. That seemed like cheating.

"I've never taught anyone in my life," said the woodcarver, "but I like you, and I'll try. I won't promise a week or a month or a year. Maybe the lesson will last only an hour. If you're willing to understand that, we can try."

"Thank you, sir. I am willing," said the young man.

They went into the studio where pieces of uncarved wood still lay, and the woodcarver said, "Pick the piece you'd like to start with, but choose it carefully."

"And how shall I know which? Shall we start big or small?"

"That I cannot say. Listen to the wood. Touch it. Watch it. Take your time, and if you can find the piece that is right for you, then perhaps we'll have another lesson."

The young man walked around and around the studio. Then he sat. He sat with his eyes open and with his eyes closed. He picked up some of the wood and then put it down. Then he noticed a small gnarled piece, almost like a scrap. This was the one he wanted.

"This is the one," he said to the woodcutter.

"And why that one?" his teacher asked.

"I cannot say for sure. But somehow I know it is this one."

"If that is so, " said the teacher, "you have chosen well."

Now the teacher looked at the small misshapen piece of wood, and he could see nothing in it, but he asked, "My boy, when you look at the wood, what do you see?"

"A baby, his sleeping head resting in the palm of a mother's hand."

The teacher remembered when he too could see such things, and he marveled at the vision of his student.

"The lesson is over for today," said the woodcarver. "Take the vision you have had, live with it, sleep with it, dream with it; then come again tomorrow."

That night sleep came more quickly than usual for the woodcarver, and in the morning he awoke with some desire to see the new day and the student who had come the day before.

"We will put the wood aside just for now," said the woodcarver, "and I will show you the tools. We will work with one tool at a time until you know it. If your hands do not know the craft, than you can never make the wood look as you see it in your vision."

The student was clumsy at first. But his teacher was patient with him. He would not have been patient had he been the great woodcarver he once was, when the craft was so easy it came to him as in a dream. He was patient because he taught as if he, too, were a novice, discovering the secrets of the craft. And he really was like a novice; though his mind remembered and he used the words of memory, his hands no longer knew the secrets.

But soon a strange thing began to happen to the woodcarver. He would coach his student during the day, watching, patiently correcting. Then at night, after the student left, he would secure a slab of wood in a vice, and he would practice with his left hand as he had instructed the student to do. At first it was as if his left hand had been born with none of the dexterity or grace of the right, but in time, he tamed it. And in time, too, the student learned to handle the tools and get them to do what he wished.

"Now," said the woodcarver, "it is time to find the sleeping child in the gnarled piece of wood. You have the tools, but the vision is your own. I will watch you, but I will not correct you. Go where you will and learn as you go. Your own mistakes will tell you more than I can. Accept them as your greatest teachers now."

He watched as the student carved into the wood, and it was like a miracle before his eyes: a tiny head emerged, the fingers of a hand, a body curving with the motion of the wood. The carving wasn't perfect, of course, but it had life and promise.

"You have done well, my boy," said the woodcarver. "Now look at the carving and tell me what worked for you and what you might do differently another time."

The young man did so, spurred on by his discoveries to try his hand at another carving.

Meanwhile, the woodcutter too was ready—at least his left hand had learned what his right had once known, but still when he looked at the wood, he saw only wood and not the beings in the wood that had guided his hand before. Nor did he feel the desire to create that had once fed his art.

HE WAS perplexed but not angry or discouraged when another stranger knocked at the door. He was a blind man.

"I have heard that you are a teacher. You can see that I am blind, but if you would be patient with me, I believe that my hands could learn the craft of woodcarving."

The woodcarver looked at the man's hands, beautiful hands with long slender fingers, just the type of hands he would have carved into the sculpture of an archer once long ago.

"I will try," said the woodcarver, "for though I have the use of my eyes, I, too, am blind." And for the first time, he revealed his secret loss.

The woodcarver taught the blind man how to use each tool, just as he had taught his first student. This man learned even more rapidly than the first. And then the time came for him to make his carving.

"Here in my studio are many pieces of wood. Explore them with your hands and find the piece you would like to carve. I cannot tell you what to carve, for though I have taught you the craft of the tools, I cannot teach you the art. That is yours alone."

The blind man examined the wood with his hands until he found a piece he wanted, and he began to carve. As the woodcutter watched, again he saw the miracle happen, for out of the wood he saw a hand emerge holding a heart.

"You are a great teacher, " said the blind man, "and I understand now how to carve. I have carved this piece for you because I know you, too, have lost your vision. But what you do not know is that you now see with your heart. Let your heart show you where to go, and perhaps your left hand will lead you there."

"Thank you," said the woodcutter, yet he was still perplexed.

That night the woodcarver chose a piece of wood to see what would happen. He did not know at first what his hand would do, but he wasn't afraid. He began to chip away and suddenly he knew what to do, not because of the vision in the wood, but from a feeling that he could not name. And the miracle happened again. Out of the wood two hands emerged: one old, gnarled, lined; the other smooth and outstretched.

And as he looked at this creation he realized that he could carve again—perhaps not as before, but that no longer troubled him. A new passion had taken the place of the old.

He was a teacher now.

STORYTELLING
and the SPIRIT *of the*
TEACHER

·÷·

*Good teachers possess a capacity for connectedness. They
are able to weave a complex web of connections among
themselves, their subjects, and their students so that students can learn to weave a world for themselves. . . . The
connections made by good teachers are held not in their
methods but in their hearts—meaning heart in its ancient
sense, as the place where intellect and emotion and spirit
will converge in the human self.*
- from *The Courage to Teach, Exploring the Inner
Landscape of a Teacher's Life* by Parker J. Palmer

IN WRITING this book I have broken down the ways that
storytelling affects the learning process in order to understand them better, isolating the impact of storytelling on
relationships, imagination, and literacy. And yet, when we tell
stories, all of this learning happens simultaneously.

That is because of a single thread that runs through
every authentic storytelling experience—the ability of a story
to create connection. Story connects teller to listener; it connects the present to the past; it connects people to cultural
traditions and values; it connects learners to knowledge; it
connects strangers and friends; it connects listeners to
thoughts and feelings—their own and others; it connects us

to our common humanity.

The simple energy that runs along this conduit of connection is emotion itself. To make connections, the storyteller/teacher must convey the emotions in the story, feelings that the teller and listeners know to be true and real, whether or not the story actually happened. Children hear authentic feeling in our voices, and they respond to it. With every story we tell, we make a deep personal connection to our students.

If students are lucky, they have a teacher sometime in their lives with whom they have truly connected—teachers who help them to learn about themselves and the world. Storytelling is one way that we can hone this ability to create connection.

I have been a teacher all my life and believe that teaching is the most rewarding, challenging, and difficult job in the world. Sometimes the pressures from the outside—rigid requirements, endless testing, and the need for students to have mastery of enormous amounts of information—make us forget what is really important to us and why we came to teaching in the first place. They make us forget the joy in learning, the spark of curiosity, the creative potential in every child. Sometimes they even make us forget our spirits and the spirits of our children.

School reform models that tell us exactly what to do without allowing us to respond to students' needs shut down our spirits. School administrators who require that we teach to tests, not to children, rob us of the creativity that allows us to respond to the organic and fluid process of working with children and ideas. Inflexible curriculum that does not permit us to meet children where they are, does not enable us to be who we are.

Those of us who choose teaching as a career do so because we wish to give something of ourselves.

We mingle a love for books and knowledge with a desire to connect with other people, sharing our enthusiasms and passions. Students who are fortunate enough to study with teachers who carry this passion often find it rubs off on them. They connect to the teacher, and through him/her they learn to connect to the subject. If they're lucky, they carry with them the love for a certain book or the curiosity about a certain subject that continues to grow, even after they leave the teacher.

The desire to tell stories has a great deal in common with the passion to teach, for both are gifts of the self which cannot be measured monetarily, despite the fact that we are paid for our labors. They are gifts of the spirit, and when we are in sync with our love for a subject or a story, we must pass it on. For as Lewis Hyde teaches in his anthropological study of gift-giving, "When a gift is used, it is not used up. Quite the opposite in fact: the gift that is not used will be lost, while the one that is passed along remains abundant."

In traditional cultures a gift is something that circulates. If we do not share it, it dies. Likewise, people with a special talent must share that talent with others. Only by giving it away, does it "remain abundant."

The mythology and folklore that have been passed down to us are free gifts from the past. They live on the breath of the spoken word, and those of us who share the stories keep them alive. We are gifted in receiving them and gifted in being able to have them live within us. But they are not truly gifts until we pass them along. Once they move, we have no control over what becomes of them. We must let them go, and the learner who takes them will transform them in his or her way, incorporating them into a way of being, believing, and living.

Although telling stories is not the only way to reclaim our spirits for teaching, it is one of the ways we can do so. In stories we can impart knowledge, uncover wisdom, and invest our hearts and spirits to inspire children to listen, to learn, to ask questions, and to search for truth.

My friend Ann Lee Brown, a wonderful weaver of the personal tale, once told me that her grandmother memorized poetry and used to say: "While you are young, fill your mind with beautiful words for they will stay with you and warm your heart as you grow older."

When we tell stories we give children a beautiful gift with the power to last a lifetime.

PART VI

ON BECOMING
a STORYTELLER

The STORYTELLER

THERE WAS once a king who loved beautiful things. He was loyal only to beauty, and he demanded the most beautiful of everything he thought of. The finest crown encrusted with jewels of every color. The grandest dance floor inlaid with precious wood in swirling designs. Intricate stained glass windows round the turret in the throne room. A flower garden which never stopped blooming.

And then, when his wife was about to bear a child, he commanded that the child be the most enchantingly beautiful the kingdom had ever seen, for this child was to inherit all the beauty in the world one day and must be worthy of it. What's more, the king's eye had grown used to beauty and could not tolerate any other sight.

After the usual nine months of waiting, the queen gave birth to a little girl. Babies often aren't very beautiful at all. They have no teeth. They have no hair. And when they cry their little faces become all twisted and red. This baby was no different.

Had the king been wise, he would have known that beauty is only one of the myriad gifts that may be given to us at birth. There are hundreds of others that lie within us like secrets. As we grow, we discover them if we're lucky. For one it may be a quick ear for a tune; for another the knack for mixing a cake just right; one may have a head for ciphering and another for poetry.

Though she lacked the gift of beauty, this young princess had been given another gift at birth. But her father the king could not see it. Nor could anyone else.

And so she grew. She crawled and walked, babbled and talked like most young children. She grew hair and teeth. But as time passed, one could see that she was not a handsome child at all, but quite homely.

The king was not at all sure what to do at first. He kept the child hidden from himself and his court. Fortunately for the little princess, her mother loved her anyway with all her heart and seemed not to notice her common features.

Though the king may have been vain and unwise, he wasn't cruel. He didn't have the princess drowned or locked in a dungeon. Instead he sent her to live in a cottage at the edge of the kingdom with her mother and her grandmother and far far from his sight and the sight of his servants and subjects. He gave them goats and chickens, and they were able to sell eggs and milk and provide for themselves.

He also wrapped in a kerchief a perfectly carved ruby. Placing this in his wife's hand, he said, "I give you this jewel on one condition: you must never tell the princess that I am her father."

Then the king returned to his palace thinking to himself, "What cannot be seen is easily forgotten."

As the princess grew up, she loved their little house at the edge of the forest. As far as she knew, this was how life was and always had been. She did not remember that she had once lived in a castle; nor did she recall anything about her father. When she grew older she asked, "Where is my father?" and her mother told her, "He died just after you were born. But he left us this house and a way to earn a living. We must be grateful for what we have."

The princess knew from her mother's eyes that this was not the whole truth about her father; yet, like many young children, she had the wisdom to know that her mother would answer no questions. "Some day I will discover a bigger truth, " she told herself and tucked away the promise to herself until the time she might be old enough to find it.

The princess loved the forest that was her backyard as much as she loved their little home. Her grandmother knew the secrets of the forest, and they would go out together and hunt for herbs and discover the hiding places of the chipmunks and the frogs.

In the spring she searched for the first flowers, and she could sit so long she thought she could actually see the tree buds turn into leaves and the flower petals unfold. While she sat there, still as a statue, birds would come and perch on her hand. At home her mother taught her how to read, and at night and on cold days she read stories to herself and to her mother and grandmother.

As she grew older, the stories she read made the princess curious. The forest had long since revealed all its secrets to her; much as she loved it, still she wished to see the world beyond its boundaries. And though she enjoyed the company of her mother and grandmother, she longed to meet other people, too.

"If you wish to see the world," her grandmother said, "you have our blessing. But please come back and tell us your stories when you have worn out your shoes and the desire for adventure."

"That I will, grandmother," she promised.

Her mother took out an old handkerchief, unwrapped it and said, "Here. Take this perfect stone. It was your father's. Should you ever be in need, you may sell it."

"Thank you, mother," she said, and she examined the jewel, holding it up to the sun, feeling the smoothness in her hand. "Ah, so my father must have been a wealthy man to have a jewel such as this, " she thought. "Perhaps this is a link to his story." She wrapped it carefully and sewed it into a pocket inside her dress, knowing that a day might come when she would be hungry or far from home and in need of its help. The jewel gave her confidence that she could go out into the world and somehow find her way home again.

With a satchel of food and a little money to get started, the princess stopped first at the nearest town and wandered through the marketplace. Hers was a new face in a village that knew all its faces by heart, and the merchants beckoned her. An old woman selling apples and raspberries called to her, "Come and sit awhile and tell me news of the world beyond this village."

"I know little of the world," said the princess, "for I am only just on my way to learn of it."

Then looking into the eyes of the old fruit seller, she asked, "Why are you so sad?"

"But child, I am smiling. What makes you think I'm sad?"

"Behind your smile, I see in your eyes a chip of sadness, old and buried, yet there just the same."

And then she was suddenly embarrassed for being so bold. "Forgive me. I am used to being only with my mother and grandmother, and I suppose in your warmth to me, you reminded me of them. I should not have spoken so freely."

"No, child. You are right. I have a sadness inside me, though it is rarely noticed. My father left one day when I was a child, and I never saw him again. No one said a word. I waited and I waited and this sorrow has lived with me like a splinter deep inside my heart. Did you realize before, my child, that you can read faces?"

"No," said the princess, "I don't think so."

"You have seen into my heart, and so I can see into yours as well. You are young, my dear, but you have the eyes of a seer. You can look into people's eyes and see the truth in their hearts. That is a gift given to few, and you need great wisdom to use it well."

The princess was humble and had no sense of her own powers. She had been isolated from the world, and if this power of seeing were truly hers, she'd had little chance to practice it. "What then do I do with this gift, if it is really as you say?"

The old woman spoke slowly, and the princess listened, as if she were carving the words into her own heart.

"Some people cannot bear to know the real truth. If you tell it to them, they refuse to hear; worse still, they may blame you for what you see. You must be careful how you share what you know with them. Some people are waiting to know what someone wiser can tell them; to them you can be a healer. Some people do not know that they have a hidden lesson to learn; to them, if they choose to listen, you can be a teacher."

"And this gift you say I have. . .do I use it to earn my bread or do I hold it inside me like a secret?"

"If you need to make your way in the world, you may use your gift to find sustenance—food and shelter. But if you use it to gain wealth beyond your needs, then the gift will begin to diminish. When money becomes more important than wisdom, wisdom will move out and find itself another home."

The princess sat quietly after that, looking at the people in the marketplace. And as she looked at them, she saw stories in their faces, stories half-hidden, half-revealed.

And then she had an idea.

She removed the ruby from the place she'd sewn in her dress. She looked across the dirt road at a man sitting beside his baskets. In his eyes she saw a sparkle, a joy, and a hint of sadness, too. Then holding the ruby in front of her eyes, she could see his story: his long and happy marriage, the loss of his beloved wife, the living grandchild he would soon be going home to see.

She put the ruby back in her skirt and sat a long time, thinking about this gift she'd never known she had: to read the stories in people's faces.

We are born with many gifts—and except for beauty—most are invisible to the eye. Some we discover in early childhood and others stay hidden for a long time. Yet even when we find our gifts, we may not know how to use them.

The princess did not know what to do with this gift of seeing, for surely it was not meant for her alone.

The next day she moved on to another town, meeting and talking with people along the way, learning about the world she had only read about in books. She had a little money which she used up after a few weeks, and she knew that she must find a way to earn enough for her food and lodging.

She set up a table in a marketplace and placed the ruby in its center. Then she wrote a sign that said: "STORYTELLER: Listen to the story of your life."

At first people passed by her table quickly, or read her sign from a distance and moved away in distrust. But a young woman with more curiosity than fear finally sat down beside the princess and said, "Why would I want to hear my own life's story? Isn't that a story I already know?"

"Perhaps," said the princess, "and perhaps not. Sometimes your own life is like a dream you cannot remember."

"And what would I pay you to hear my own story?"

"Whatever you can spare for my dinner and a night's sleep."

"Fair enough," said the young woman.

Looking through her ruby the princess told the young woman the story of her life, and as she listened, the woman heard pieces she'd been missing, pieces she'd forgotten somehow. Though it was her own life, it was as if she'd misplaced it along the way and had suddenly rediscovered it.

"I've always loved other people's stories," she told the princess, "but I didn't know I had a story. You have returned to me something that is mine. Thank you. Seeing the past, I know better where I'm going."

The princess traveled in this way from town to town, earning enough to live. When she told people their own stories, it was as if they saw their lives appear like a tapestry being woven before their eyes. And they'd walk away then with the whole cloth of their lives, remembered again.

Word of the seer spread through the kingdom, for no one had ever before met anyone with her special powers. Even the king heard about the woman who could tell stories of people's lives.

The king had grown old, and he had lost his eyesight. The pleasure he had gotten from the beautiful objects was gone, and all he found now was emptiness. Yet when he heard about the storyteller, he discovered in himself a great desire to know her, though he could not say why.

When the princess came to the castle, she did not feel fear; she was not overwhelmed by magnificence. Indeed, the place seemed somehow familiar, and she wondered why. And when she was brought before the king, she did not feel herself in the presence of power or greatness; she saw only an old man, a pitiful old man.

Holding up the precious ruby before her eyes, she looked into the king's eyes. The king could not see the shining jewel, for he was blind.

"Your majesty," she said softly, "you have been blinded by beauty. Your whole life long, you saw only the surface of things. You drank in color, the magnificence of stained glass and flowers. Now you think you are blind, but you are not. Perhaps you still have time to learn to see."

"Many years ago your wife gave birth to a daughter. You could only see her face, and that face did not please you. You sent her far away from you. Do you remember?"

"Yes, I remember now. What happened to the child? Can you tell me?"

"Your eyes can tell only your story and do not know hers. I cannot tell you what you have never known," said the princess.

"I would have a clue, perhaps," he said. "I gave her mother a perfectly carved ruby on the condition that she never tell the princess that I was her father. Perhaps somehow we could find the ruby."

The princess listened and knew the truth. Her truth. Not his.

"Perhaps some day you can find your daughter if you can learn to see—not with your eyes—but through the window of your soul."

"Since I've lost my sight," said the king, "I thought all windows were closed to me. I have sat here in silence, waiting for the next ending. Where is that window you speak of?"

"If you would like," said the princess, "I will stay here a while and help you to see in a different way."

The king readily agreed.

Every day the princess took the king into the forest. She remembered the lessons of her grandmother, and she taught the king to listen to the sounds of birds and distinguish amongst them. He felt the moss, learned the herbs through their scent and shape. Sometimes he asked the princess to tell him stories of other people's lives, stories that had never held any interest before, and now he loved them. He loved the sound of her voice. He loved her as he had never loved anyone.

"I wish you were my daughter," he said one day.

Taking the perfect ruby from the secret pocket in her dress, the princess laid it in his hand. "I am," she said, "for you have learned to see me."

WHEN THE princess returned to her mother and grandmother at the edge of the kingdom, she walked slowly, for she was guiding a blind old man.

Just as she'd promised, she told them story after story.
The very last one she told was this one.

FINDING YOUR
STORYTELLING VOICE

⋅⋅⋅

A LTHOUGH THERE are many excellent resources for developing your skills as a storyteller, it is most helpful to begin by taking a workshop. Having a guide and an interactive group will give you the hands–on tools you need to begin. Finding opportunities to watch other storytellers will also give you many ideas. Practice, listen, and watch: these are the three key elements to learning the art of storytelling.

As you begin to develop your repertoire on your own, here are some suggestions you might wish to keep in mind:

- Select only material that draws you. If you choose a story because you think your students will like it even though you don't really like it yourself, you won't have any real motivation to tell it. On the other hand, if you select a story that you love, you will captivate your audience because of your personal commitment to the material.

- You will need to read many stories to find the ones which speak to you. If you're interested in reading folktales, browse in the 398.2 section of your library.

- Once you find a tale that you like, you can find other published versions (the same tale told by a different writer) and variants (a story with similar motifs, often from another culture) of the story by looking at a motif index called *The Storyteller's Source Book* by Margaret

Read MacDonald. Finding other versions of the story you wish to tell can help you create your own retelling of the story.

- Unless your story is a literary tale which requires mastery of the text, try not to memorize the text of your tale. Make it your own.

As you tell a story, if you feel as if you are living in the story, you will create a magical experience for the listeners; they will be right there with you. You can try some of the following simple exercises to help locate yourself inside the world of the story:

- Move through the story with your eyes closed, picturing everything that happens as the characters see it.
- Make an audio tape of the story and listen to it with your eyes closed in order to be able to picture the landscapes.
- Be sure you know the sequence of events very clearly. This does not require memorization. It is just a quick review of what happens in the story. You can check yourself by making a quick list or sketching the events.
- Meditate upon what draws you to the story. It may be a theme, the humor, a character, an image, a bit of dialogue, or a particular incident or interaction. Often that is the gift inside the story for you, and the one you will be giving to your audience. You don't need to "tell" them what the gift is, but the treasure will come in the way you deliver the story.
- When you tell the story, if a character has the opportunity to speak, put the language into dialogue. In other words, it is not effective to say, "The woodcutter said that he was hungry." Instead say, "The woodcutter said, 'I'm very hungry'."

- When you speak from the point of view of the character, feel as if you really are that character. This means that you must truly identify with the emotions that the character is feeling. An effective and powerful telling is almost completely dependent upon authentic emotional connection. You can't pretend or guess what the character might be feeling and create an imitation. That will feel superficial both to teller and listener. But if you can truly identify with the character, the emotion will come through authentically. Each time you actually tell the story, you will find that the intensity of emotion will vary, depending upon you and your audience. In order to be real and true to the story, be flexible and respond to the story as it comes to you, without forcing it to be something you do not feel.

- Since I like to write, after I've worked on the story for a while in movement and visualization, I like to write my own version. This usually becomes the text that I work from. It helps me discover the language I want to use. If you enjoy writing, try to write your version of the story.

- When I'm just at the brink of being able to tell a story, I like to sit alone in a closed room and tell it to myself with my eyes closed. Being alone takes away the self-consciousness of being hesitant or unsure of my material. Having my eyes closed allows me to visualize the story. This gives me my first notion of where I am with the story. How much of it feels comfortable and natural? What do I still need to work on?

- When you finally share the story with an audience, try to be totally in the moment with the story. If you are true to the story and yourself at the same time, you will find that no two presentations are ever the same. Each telling of a story is a complete and inimitable experience.

To find out more about the Storytelling Arts institutes for teachers, visit www.storytellingarts.net. To explore general information about storytelling resources around the United States, visit the National Storytelling Network at www.storynet.org.

APPENDIX
Notes on the Stories

OF THE SIX stories included in this book, three are my retellings of traditional folktales and three are stories I have written. Since folktales are originally told orally, most storytellers find versions of a story they like and craft their own version. If you like these tales, you may wish to consult other versions.

"The Tiger's Whisker" and "The Lion's Whisker" can be found in these collections:

Ashabranner, Brent. *The Lion's Whisker and Other Ethiopian Tales*. Linnet Books, 1997.

Courlander, Harold. *The Tiger's Whisker and Other Tales and Legends from Asia and the Pacific*. Harcourt, Brace, Janovich, Inc. 1959.

Day, Nancy Raines. *The Lion's Whiskers*. Scholastic, 1995.

Holt, David and Bill Mooney. *Ready-to-tell-Tales*. August House, 1994.

"The Lost Child" can be found in this collection:

Nic Leodhas, Sorche. *Thistle and Thyme*. Holt Rinehart and Winston, 1962.

"The Magic Brocade" can be found in these collections:

Batt, Tanya Robyn. *The Fabrics of Fairytale*. Barefoot Books, 2000.

Cole, Joanna. *Best-loved Folktales of the World.* Doubleday, 1982.

Heyer, Marilee. *The Weaving of a Dream.* Viking Kestrel, 1986.

Jagendorf, M.A. and Virginia Weng. *The Magic Boat.* Vanguard, 1980.

Liyi, He. *The Spring of Butterflies.* Lothrop, 1988.

A literary fairytale is an original story that resembles the folktale or fairytale in its voice and form. The following are my stories:

"The Forgotten Gifts" © 1992
"The Vision in the Wood" © 1995
"The Storyteller" © 1995 ("The Seer")

SOURCES CITED:

Part I:

MacDonald, Margaret Read. *The Storyteller's Sourcebook.* Gale, 1982 and 2001.

Shedlock, Marie. *The Art of the Story-Teller.* D. Appleton and Company, NY, 1915.

Part II:

McDermott, Raymond P. "Social Relations as Contexts for Learning in School." *Harvard Educational Review.* Volume 47 (1977), pp.198-213.

Part III:

Burnett, Frances Hodgson. *The Little Princess.* (This book was first published in 1905 and is available in many editions.)

Carson, Rachel. *A Sense of Wonder.* Harper and Row, 1956.

Gardner, John. *The Art of Fiction, Notes on Craft for Young Writers.* Alfred A. Knopf, Inc., 1983. (p. 73)

Sewall, Laura. "Reversing the World," *Orion.* Autumn 1999.

Tolkien, J.R.R. "Children and Fairy Stories." In *Only Connect, Readings on Children's Literature,* Edited by Egoff, Stubbs, et.al. Oxford University Press, 1996.

Part IV:

Keene, Ellin Oliver and Susan Zimmerman.
Mosaic of Thought. Heinemann, 1997.

Purcell-Gates, Victoria. *Other People's Words,
The Cycle of Low Literacy.* Harvard University Press, 1997.

Welty, Eudora. *One Writer's Beginnings.*
Harvard University Press, 1984.

Part V:

Hyde, Lewis. *The Gift.* Vintage Books, 1983.

Palmer, Parker. *The Courage to Teach, Exploring the Inner
Landscape of a Teacher's Life.* Jossey-Bass, 1998.

Susan Danoff has told stories and taught storytelling and writing for many years. She is founder and Executive Director of Storytelling Arts, Inc., and she teaches the Storytelling Arts summer institutes. Susan has produced three audio recordings—*Enchantments, The Invisible Way: Stories of Wisdom, and Women of Vision*—which can be downloaded from her website. She lives with her husband and son in Princeton, New Jersey.

www.susandanoff.com
susan@storytellingarts.net

Storytelling Arts, Inc., provides long-term storytelling programs for low-income and special needs school children and their teachers in New Jersey in order to strengthen literacy skills and motivation for learning. Storytelling Arts also offers pre-service and in-service workshops for teachers at all levels. Weeklong summer institutes at Princeton University draw teachers from all over the country.

www.storytellingarts.net
info@storytellingarts.net